Shalom Series

ACTIVATING THE POWER OF PASTORAL CARE

A TEAM APPROACH

Rev Dr My B Jer

By Rev. Dr. Mary B. Johnson

"Carry each other's burdens, and in this way you will fulfill the law of Christ." -Galatians 6:2

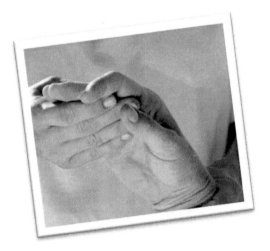

"For I, the LORD your God, hold your right hand; it is I who say to you, "Fear not, I am the one who helps you." -Isaiah 41:13

ACTIVATING THE POWER OF PASTORAL CARE: A TEAM APPROACH

By Rev. Dr. Mary B. Johnson

Good News Publishing International

GNSM, Inc.

PO Box 10212, Swanzey, NH 03446

Published in the United States Of America

Cover, book design, and Illustration by author
Any graphics not original are from public domain

ISBN-13:978-0692629246
ISBN-10:0692629246

DEDICATION

This book is dedicated with appreciation to all Pastoral Care givers who have labored long and faithfully in the harvest fields of life with a generous heart and compassionate spirit in the face of challenging times and difficult days. May the many faithful pastoral care givers be blessed even as they have so deeply blessed others. Special appreciation is extended to Rev. Dennis Marquardt, Rev. Dr. David Abbott, Rev. Ray Hodgeney, Rev. Jackie Brannen, Rev. Diane Bennett, Rev. Ken Borchers, Rev. Ann Nelson, Rev. Pat Rainey, Pastor Arnie Johnson, Pat & Joe Tonweber, Pastor Aaron Cox, Rev. Elizabeth Davis, Lillian Snellman, R.N., Dr. Phyllis Porter, R.N. and the Peterborough/West Rindge, NH UMC Pastoral Care Team for their courage, dedication, hard work, faithfulness, compassion, and wisdom in the challenging areas of pastoral and crisis care.

TABLE OF CONTENTS

Activating The Power of Pastoral Care:

A Team Approach

PART 1: BUILDING MINISTRY TEAMS

PART 2:

CRISIS CARE: THE ART AND SKILLS OF CRISIS COUNSELING

Activating The Power of Pastoral Care

A TEAM APPROACH

PART 1

Building Ministry

Teams

By

Rev. Dr. Mary B. Johnson

"Give yourself fully to God. He will use you to accomplish great things on the condition that you believe much more in His love than in your own weakness."
Mother Teresa

OVERVIEW

The gifts of dynamic pastoral care are enormous including healing from hopelessness, stronger marriages and families, comfort in grief and crisis, support in illness, hope in loneliness, inclusion in isolation, and light in the darkness of despair. The power of quality pastoral care to impact our communities, grow our churches, and insure healthy ministries and congregations cannot be overestimated. In an age of overwhelming complexities and challenge to our churches and society, the need for ways to expand and maintain the provision of effective Pastoral Care has become paramount. Our Mental Health Care systems are strained to the breaking point while social service organizations and state and federal programs, for those in need, have been drastically reduced in most areas. The support services that were once available have rapidly diminished while the need for healing Pastoral Care in our society, ministries, and churches has multiplied quickly with the disintegration of the nuclear and extended family. Concurrently, many pastors have received either little or inadequate training and preparation for the demanding mental health needs occurring in our complex stress filled culture. Yet in the face of this need for Pastoral Care, most pastors find themselves overworked, understaffed, and sometimes in danger of burning out. Consequently, this book and guide to establishing and maintaining expanded pastoral care services has been carefully developed in order to prepare ALL Christians including pastors, ministers, and lay people to share the dynamic power of compassionate pastoral care in a hurting world. It can be used either as an informative book by itself or as a proven effective training manual and workbook to build effective Ministry Outreach Teams utilizing team power.

These same materials have been used successfully by other churches and ministries to assist and support the senior pastor and congregation in providing the best quality of Pastoral Care possible. More importantly, *"Activating the Power of Pastoral Care"* has been used to grow churches, reach out to the community, and spread the Good News of Christ to a needy world in practical ways in our post-Christian age. It has reinvigorated a sense of meaning and purpose in local churches and engaged far more people in active ministry and outreach thereby often improving worship attendance. Ultimately however, the most important effect this book may have is to share the Good News of Christ with others and bring new people into our churches. This has and can be done by reaching outside the walls of our congregations with effective Ministry Teams that can impact hurting people with the compassion, care, concern, and healing power of Christ.

This book has been developed after decades as a pastor with extensive pastoral and clinical Mental Health experience including educating, training, developing, and mentoring Chaplains, pastors, specialized ministers, and counselors. The materials and methods presented are the practical result of both training and acting as a Consultant to effective Ministry Teams, pastors, and care givers in a number of denominational settings and a large variety of churches and ministries. When the training methods and educational materials presented in "*Activating the Power of Pastoral Care*" are adhered to, Ministry Teams have functioned well and effectively and greatly enhanced the mission, outreach, and growth of local churches and been a blessing to pastors, congregations, and communities.

Training Groups should consist of not more than 12 in each class as the team members will be working together and need to develop a mutual respect and trust with each other and the Senior Pastor. Total classroom time to complete the Training Program for Ministry Teams is approximately 12-16 hours. Eleven chapters, one for each session, are included that are designed to take around one and a half to two hours. Training time for Part 1 of the Pastoral Care part of the course is approximately 8 hours and an additional 8 hours for Part 2 on Crisis Care. It is recommended training sessions be no less than one and a half hours per individual session in order for questions to be adequately answered. Some groups have found that, in order to complete the training, a series of 3 or 4 Saturday educational sessions has worked well of 5 to 6 hours per session. Others have arranged a series of midweek evening sessions form 6:30-8:00 PM. Do what works best for your situation. All sessions should begin and end with a brief prayer.

A local Pastoral Care Team can be functioning and operating after Part 1 has been completed, if desired. Part 2 is designed to enhance and broaden the basic skills learned in Part 1. Extensive Power Point presentations may be available to supplement training by contacting the author at booksbymbj@gmail.com. However, this book stands alone as a complete resource. Each student will need their own book which can also serve as their personal workbook. For ease of use, color coding is used with "Questions" sections highlighted in blue."Case Studies" are highlighted in brown and "Group Activities" in green. If this book is used primarily to train Ministry Teams, care should be given that questions and case studies are ALSO discussed in group. Otherwise, training will not be as effective and some can feel overwhelmed or discouraged when engaged in real visitations. Materials in Appendix sections are examples only but may be locally adapted.

It is recommended, if possible, that a Consultant with a degree and/or experience in some aspect of Mental Health and/or Pastoral Care training also be present for part or all of the training. This can include either a Social Worker, Nurse, Counselor, Physician, Chaplain, or other appropriate people. In order for a Ministry Team to function at its optimum, an eventual organizational pattern usually emerges that has a Leadership Team consisting of a gifted lay person to act as a Pastoral Care Team Coordinator, a Senior Pastor in charge, and a Consultant available for varying degrees of consultation regarding the more challenging Pastoral Care and Mental Health issues that arise in our complex society. The Pastoral Care Team is designed to work respectfully and cooperatively with the Senior Pastor and should be under the overall guidance and authority of the church or ministry they represent at all times.

Shalom, Rev. Dr. Mary B. Johnson

Chapter 1: **Pastoral Gifts**

BUILDING PASTORAL CARE TEAMS

"There is a greater poverty in the West than the poverty of hunger in the East. It is the poverty of loneliness that destroys the soul. Being unwanted, unloved, uncared for, forgotten by everybody, I think that is a much greater hunger, a much greater poverty than the person who has nothing to eat. I am not sure exactly what heaven will be like, but I don't know that when we die and it comes time for God to judge us, he will NOT ask, "How many good things have you done in your life?" Rather he will ask, "How much LOVE did you put into what you did?" Mother Teresa

The power of effective pastoral care to transform our world, grow our churches, and bring healing comfort and renewal to our communities is unlimited. However, pastoral care is increasingly misunderstood and underutilized or restricted to ordained clergy. There is great confusion and debate among ministries, churches, and congregations today in our post modern age as to how we can even best define or understand Pastoral Care. Theologically, it can be defined as the "care and cure of souls". Yet, the practical working definition of **Pastoral Care** is fairly basic and is perhaps best understood as *"the caring actions of a Christian, gifted with pastoral gifts by the Holy Spirit, who is called to a ministry of love, caring, guidance, nurturing, protection, healing and compassion. This ministry is for the benefit of others in order to care for all people in need without discrimination, build up the Body of Christ, and establish the church and community as a safe and secure place enabling each individual to grow and mature into all Christ has called us to be."*

The transformational and healing abilities of pastoral care are unique with multiple opportunities to bring healing that are not offered in counseling, psychotherapy, medicine, social work, or any other profession including:

- ❖ Access to the homes of parishioners so that pastoral care and pastoral counseling can be done in context;
- ❖ A previously established relationship of trust which is critical to effective care that can bring a deeper healing;

- ❖ Access to people in pivotal times of crisis and change including relational difficulties, weddings, divorce, birth, baptisms, death, bereavement, loss, sickness, and hardship;
- ❖ The opportunity to offer care, counsel, healing, and wisdom without complicated written contracts and the necessity of monetary transactions and insurance forms.

Such opportunities are priceless in our complex society to being healing, growth, wisdom, sound counsel, and stability to individuals, families, and communities. However, the privilege of walking through the soul of another is a sacred one and calls for the highest ethical standards that respects the confidentiality, privacy, and integrity of those who entrust their inmost needs and vulnerability to our imperfect perspectives. At the same time, the opportunities for celebration and affirmation in the significant life events of families and other individuals are diverse and currently seem unique to the office of the pastor in our society. When and where pastoral care becomes pastoral counseling can be confusing at times unless pastoral care givers remember they are not present in pastoral visits primarily for their own needs or to talk about themselves. Rather we are there for the needs and concerns of the souls entrusted to our care. The listening ears and heart of a true pastor are always attuned to seek out the hurting and lost who need a healing touch of support, concern, wise counsel, and prayer.

 However it is vital to remember Pastoral gifts are given by the Holy Spirit to both lay people and clergy. As Christians we are **ALL** called to carry out the mission of Jesus to proclaim Good News to the oppressed and "heal the broken hearted."(Lk.4:18). However, Paul's letter to the early church in Rome reminds us today of the truth, *"For just as each of us has one body with many members, and these members do not all have the same function, so in Christ we, though many, form one body, and each member belongs to all the others. We have different gifts, according to the grace given to each of us. If your gift is prophesying, then prophesy in accordance with your faith; if it is serving, then serve; if it is teaching, then teach; if it is to encourage, then give encouragement; if it is giving, then give generously; if it is to lead, do it diligently; if it is to show mercy, do it cheerfully." (Rom.12:4-8; NIV2011)*

This gifting calls us forth to serve in many kinds of ministerial capacities. The "priesthood of all believers" is a basic tenant of the Christian faith for most and opens the doors to involvement in ministries of Pastoral Care and service for all who wish to follow Jesus. Indeed, Jesus said we will know the true from the false disciples by their "love one for another." Pastoral Care and concern follows love like the light follows the Sun. However, the degree, amount, and effectiveness of Pastoral Care we find ourselves engaged in within our church, parish, and community is determined by not only our calling, but how well we are equipped and trained for this critical outreach.

In spite of our preconceptions and cultural expectations, the hard truth remains that no one Pastor is able to do all the Pastoral Care within the church body by themselves. The early church recognized this fact by appointing "deacons" to assist those in early church leadership in Pastoral Care functions and duties (Acts 6). Likewise, the wisdom that was granted to Moses was to let others "hold up his hands" to strengthen him in pastoral and leadership responsibilities in order to win many terrible battles when the Israelites were attacked by powerful enemies. Exodus gives us the perfect model of effective victorious pastoral teamwork when it tells us that: *"The Amalekites came and attacked the Israelites at Rephidim.*  *Moses said to Joshua, 'Choose some of our men and go out to fight the Amalekites. Tomorrow I will stand on top of the hill with the staff of God in my hands.' So Joshua fought the Amalekites as Moses had ordered, and Moses, Aaron, and Hur went to the top of the hill. As long as Moses held up his hands, the Israelites were winning, but whenever he lowered his hands, the Amalekites were winning. When Moses' hands grew tired, they took a stone and put it under him and he sat on it. Aaron and Hur held his hands up--one on one side, one on the other--so that his hands remained steady till sunset. So Joshua and the Israelites overcame the Amalekite army and the battle was won that day."* (Ex 17:8-13; NIV)

Many are still inspired by the example of such a dedicated and faithful team that surrounded Moses and cared for their pastor and protected the people. Such "Pastoral Care" Ministry Teams are desperately needed in our time in order to win the battle all Christians are engaged in today for the minds, hearts, and souls of people. For we live in a crumbling world of confusion, despair, increasing addictions, and moral swamps. Indeed, most journalists, scholars, and theologians are now referring to our time and age as being "post-Christian." While needs for Pastoral Care have multiplied astronomically with the breakdown of the family and our addiction-based culture, the availability and energy of overworked credentialed pastors to do the minimal basics of Pastoral Care has broken down. It seems it may be past time for the entire Christian community to return to the New Testament model of the church and once again develop and establish committed well-trained Ministry Teams to offer effective pastoral care. If Christianity is to fulfill its mission in our troubled world, we need to act quickly while opportunities are still open in a post Christian culture.

Yet if we are to do this, we must first realize that lay people are both called and gifted by the Holy Spirit for ministries but are often unsure how to begin or what to do. We need to remember that in the Gospels it was Jesus himself who modeled for us the true nature of Pastoral Care in his compassion and healing ministry. He sent out his followers into the surrounding communities as teams of two and charged the disciples on their mission to proclaim Good News and to "Heal the sick, raise the dead, cleanse those who have leprosy, drive out demons. Freely you have received, freely give." (Matt. 10:8; NIV) They were directed to carry out the same caring pastoral ministries they had seen their Lord accomplish. And so it is that the followers of Christ in our time are also called to follow the commands of our Lord to proclaim Good News and heal.

Most ordained or licensed pastors today are overwhelmed with the growing responsibilities and increasingly complex demands the *sole* responsibility brings of providing Pastoral Care in

struggling congregations. Yet the Protestant Reformation clearly taught and proclaimed the "priesthood of all believers" and the fact that we are all, as Christians, called to ministry. This book will attempt to free us from the cultural expectation that THE lone pastor is supposed to "do it all" and will offer a more effective team approach. It is designed to equip and enable ALL of us in the body of Christ to become wiser and more effective Pastoral Care givers no matter our levels of previous experience, training, or status. Working together as a team, we can release the power of pastoral care in order to transform our world for Christ! By doing so, we will be enabled to also grow our churches and bring healing and hope to people both inside and outside our ministry walls.

✓ *Questions For Individual Reflection Or Group Discussion:*

1. What kinds of skills do you feel you would need to do some of the basic types of Pastoral Care?

2. Are you more comfortable with the prospect of doing some types of Pastoral Care than others?

3. Which ones?

4. In Romans 12:4-8, as quoted in this chapter, the apostle Paul discusses some gifts of the Holy Spirit that are related to pastoral care. Do you believe you have any of these gifts? If so, please specify which ones you may have? If not, please share what ministry gifts you feel you possess that could be related to helping others.

Chapter 2: Different Types Of Pastoral Care

The gospels show Jesus as a model of Pastoral Care, meeting each person at the point of a specific need, respecting the dignity and worth of all, honoring each person's individuality and tailoring a specific response to the needs of the individual before him. It seems clear, from a careful reading of the gospels, that He intended all Christians would follow his example and become caregivers, a matter explored in the New Testament letters. Most of the letters of the New Testament were addressed to churches and a large variety of people within them and not solely to church leaders. Indeed, even a casual reading reveals that all Christians were responsible for Pastoral Care in the early church.

In the New Testament, all Christians were called to "love one another deeply, from the heart," (1 Peter 1:22; NIV) "bear with each other and forgive," (Col. 3:13; NIV) and "serve one another in love." (Galatians 5:13; NIV). As Christians we receive the comfort of God "in all our troubles, so that we can comfort those in any trouble with the comfort we ourselves have received from God." (2 Cor. 1:4; NIV) It is clear biblically then that **all** Christians have a specific responsibility to offer care to people in need. The apostolic church did not draw distinctions between the compassionate care that should be offered by all Christians and expressions of care that were only allowed by those holding a pastoral leadership "office."

Peter tells the crowds gathered at Pentecost shortly after the resurrection of Jesus that the dramatic manifestations of the Holy Spirit gifts upon the gathered crowds were *"...what was spoken by the prophet Joel: 'In the last days, God says, I will pour out my Spirit on all people. Your sons and daughters will prophesy, your young men will see visions, your old men will dream dreams. Even on my servants, both men and women, I will pour out my Spirit in those days....."* (Acts 2:16-18; NIV). Consequently, since God's Spirit in our time now dwells among his people and in each believer, every member of the church is gifted for ministry in some way. It does not ultimately matter if we can specifically identify and label all our "gifts." Gifts can vary and change over time and with the needs of our Christian community.

While one or two of our gifts may remain primary, questionnaires that enable us to identify our gifts can be very helpful. However, they may also discourage us from remaining open to the multiple ways God's Spirit might choose to manifest through us. We may even keep trying to be the "person" described and limited in the inventory. It is more important to recognize that there is a great diversity of Spirit ministry in the body of Christ. It is vital not to be limited concerning the Spirit's work in us, a work that may change from time to time. If we are confused about our "gifts," it is enough to serve one another in love. (1 Cor.13) Gifts of the Spirit are not given for personal

comfort or our own private enjoyment but for the "building up" of others. There is no lack of opportunities to do this and to encourage and comfort others just as there is no lack in the Spirit's provision for those who depend on the Lord. Diverse activities were, and are, defined as "Pastoral Care" in both the ancient and modern church. Today, Pastoral Care involves a variety of actions ranging over such areas as:

- **Phone calls, Cards, Letters, Emails to those needing comfort/ encouragement**
- **Offering wisdom, a listening ear, and understanding to those in need**
- **Counsel from a Christian and pastoral perspective**
- **Hands on Prayer for and with _specific_ people who are in need**
- **Home Visits to those in difficult situations or the lonely**
- **Providing Visits, worship services, or music to orphanages, prisons, etc.**
- **Providing food /meals or home visits to the sick or shut in**
- **Providing transportation for doctor visits or emergencies for those in need**
- **Bringing meals to the home during crisis, funerals, or loss of loved ones**
- **Nursing Home Visits to the chronically ill or elderly**
- **Hospital Visits with the sick, dying, injured, etc.**
- **Practical Assistance including meals, transportation, shelter, moving, etc.**
- **Home repairs for the infirm /needy including building handicap ramps to homes**
- **Crisis Care & Support (in bereavement, marital/family, or individual crisis)**
- **Offering shelter or protection in domestic violence, abuse, bullying, etc.**
- **Guidance in spiritual and emotional stress and confusion**
- **Appropriate Referrals to community resources when more care is needed**
- **Providing Food Banks and Homeless Shelters**

While a large variety of interactions and relationships can fall under the category of "Pastoral Care", *the basic core of Pastoral CARE is the willingness and ability to stand with others in diverse and sometimes difficult situations where we intentionally represent the larger Body Of Christ and desire to bring healing, guidance, hope, and the compassionate love of Christ to the wounded, lost, ill, or in need.* While some social interaction may occur during Pastoral Care, the primary purpose is not a social one. The needs of the other person are paramount and not our own needs. Good Pastoral Care always consists of:

Compassionate Listening & Good Communications

Appropriate Actions

Relationships that are Christ-Centered

Empathy of A Healing Nature

✓ *Questions For Individual Reflection Or Group Discussion:*

1. *What areas of pastoral care do you feel fairly confident in?*

2. *Which types of Pastoral Care do you find somewhat intimidating?*

3. *How do you think you would feel before a Pastoral Care visit to someone in crisis?*

4. *What pastoral care needs exist in your church or community?*

CASE STUDY

 It is 6PM and you have recently received word, during your dinner time, that Andrea's husband John was pronounced deceased at 5:30PM after a fatal encounter with a drunk driver while driving home from work. Andrea and John have been attending your church for the last year and have been very active and faithful in attendance, but are not church members. John and Andrea are both school teachers and have helped in the Sunday School over the past year. The doctor has called and informed you that Andrea is at the local hospital Emergency Room in shock and was mildly sedated after the news. She is now asking to see you. The doctor also informs you that their two college age sons still do not know of the fatal accident.

1. What would you do to provide Pastoral Care in this situation?

GROUP ACTIVITY

> *2. Make a comprehensive plan about ministering in this situation with others as a group as if you plan to act together as a Pastoral Care Team.*

Chapter 3: "PASTORAL" Ways Of Providing Care

The heart of what "**PASTORAL**" Care entails, as distinguished from other kinds of care, can best be understood by exploring its origins in the word "Pastor" or "to pastor" from the Hebrew word "*ro-eh*" in Hebrew, meaning "Shepherd." The Task of the "Good Shepherd" is to care for the sheep by the following means: nurturing, protecting, guarding, comforting, seeking the lost, binding up wounded, feeding, bringing home drifters, etc. Jesus is portrayed in the gospels as the "Good Shepherd" and refers to his mission and himself oftentimes in this manner. Leaders, disciples, priests, deacons, and those with Pastoral Care responsibilities are frequently referred to in the Bible as "Shepherds." God's people throughout the Bible are often referred to as "sheep." Please carefully consider the following questions for reflection as we prepare to examine some pivotal readings in this chapter based on John 10:1-21, Ezekiel, and Jeremiah. As we read the words of Jesus from John, we will be seeking to understand more deeply what a good shepherd is and what they are expected to do in the way of Pastoral Care. Ezekiel and Jeremiah provide an in depth understanding of the enormous power of good pastoral care and the terrible consequences of the lack of it in our communities.

✓ Questions For Reflection

1. What do you think it would mean to be a "good shepherd" in this day and age?

2. What practical things can we do in our own church community and neighborhoods to be, or become, "good shepherds"?

3. What happens to our Christian community and churches without enough good shepherds that are caring for the sheep?

The Good Shepherd

"I tell you the truth, the man who does not enter the sheep pen by the gate, but climbs in by some other way, is a thief and a robber. The man who enters by the gate is the shepherd of his sheep. The watchman opens the gate for him, and the sheep listen to his voice. He calls his own sheep by name and leads them out. When he has brought out all his own, he goes on ahead of them, and his sheep follow him because they know his voice. But they will never follow a stranger; in fact, they will run away from him because they do not recognize a stranger's voice." Jesus used this figure of speech, but they did not understand what he was telling them. Therefore Jesus said again, "I tell you the truth, I am the gate for the sheep. All who ever came before me were thieves and robbers, but the sheep did not listen to them. I am the gate; whoever enters through me will be saved. He will come in and go out, and find pasture. The thief comes only to steal and kill and destroy; I have come that they may have life, and have it to the full. "I am the good shepherd. The good shepherd lays down his life for the sheep. The hired hand is not the shepherd who owns the sheep. So when he sees the wolf coming, he abandons the

 sheep and runs away. Then the wolf attacks the flock and scatters it. The man runs away because he is a hired hand and cares nothing for the sheep. "I am the good shepherd; I know my sheep and my sheep know me-- just as the Father knows me and I know the Father--and I lay down my life for the sheep. I have other sheep that are not of this sheep pen. I must bring them also. They too will listen to my voice, and there shall be one flock and one shepherd. The reason my Father loves me is that I lay down my life--only to take it up again. No one takes it from me, but I lay it down of my own accord. I have authority to lay it down and authority to take it up again. This command I received from my Father." At these words the Jews were again divided. Many of them said, "He is demon-possessed and raving mad. Why listen to him?" But others said, "These are not the sayings of a man possessed by a demon. Can a demon open the eyes of the blind?" (John 10:1-21; NIV)

Bad and Good Shepherds

In a larger Biblical context, we can conclude the Good Shepherd presented in *John 10* stands in contrast to the blind leaders that had been referred to in John *9:41* (Sadducees, Pharisees, etc.) who were probably, in reality, the ones also referred to as "Satan's children" in John 8:44. It seems John intended Chapter 10 on "The Good Shepherd" to be a part of the revelation of the full meaning of Jesus as a model for our own lives as his disciples. For a full understanding of the importance of providing good "Pastoral Care," Jesus' discourse on the "Good Shepherd" in John needs to be carefully studied and understood in light of the numerous Old Testament references to "good" and "bad" human shepherds. (cf. Ps. 23:1; Isa. 40:11; 56:9-12; Jer. 23:1-4; Ezek. 34:23; Zech.11:1-17). Jesus used this familiar pastoral and rural image of the "Shepherd" to communicate important truths regarding himself and our purpose and duties as his disciples. However, for a clearer understanding of the Pastoral Care we are called to emulate as "good shepherds," we also need to carefully compare John 10 with additional texts from the OT prophets Jeremiah and Ezekiel following in the next pages.

Jeremiah

Jeremiah 23:1-4 (NIV): [1] "Woe to the shepherds who are destroying and scattering the sheep of my pasture!" declares the LORD. [2] Therefore this is what the LORD, the God of Israel, says to the shepherds who tend my people: "Because you have scattered my flock and driven them away and have not bestowed care on them, I will bestow punishment on you for the evil you have done," declares the LORD. [3] "I myself will gather the remnant of my flock out of all the countries where I have driven them and will bring them back to their pasture, where they will be fruitful and increase in number. [4] I will place shepherds over them who will tend them, and they will no longer be afraid or terrified, nor will any be missing," declares the LORD. "

Ezekiel

Ezekiel 34:1-16 (NIV): "The word of the LORD came to me: [2] "Son of man, prophesy against the shepherds of Israel; prophesy and say to them: 'This is what the Sovereign LORD says: Woe to the shepherds of Israel who only take care of themselves! Should not shepherds take care of the

flock? [3] You eat the curds, clothe yourselves with the wool and slaughter the choice animals, but you do not take care of the flock. [4] You have not strengthened the weak or healed the sick or bound up the injured. You have not brought back the strays or searched for the lost. You have ruled them harshly and brutally. [5] So they were scattered because there was no shepherd, and when they were scattered they became food for all the wild animals. [6] My sheep wandered over all the mountains and on every high hill. They were scattered over the earth, and no one searched or looked for them.

[7] "'Therefore, you shepherds, hear the word of the LORD: [8] As surely as I live, declares the Sovereign LORD, because my flock lacks a shepherd and so has been plundered and has become food for all the wild animals, and because my shepherds did not search for my flock but cared for themselves rather than for my flock, [9] therefore, O shepherds, hear the word of the LORD: [10] This is what the Sovereign LORD says: I am against the shepherds and will hold them accountable for my flock. I will remove them from tending the flock so that the shepherds can no longer feed themselves. I will rescue my flock from their mouths, and it will no longer be food for them. [11] "'For this is what the Sovereign LORD says: I myself will search for my sheep and look after them. [12] As a shepherd looks after his scattered flock when he is with them, so will I look after my sheep. I will rescue them from all the places where they were scattered on a day of clouds and darkness. [13] I will bring them out from the nations and gather them from the countries, and I will bring them into their own land. I will pasture them on the mountains of Israel, in the ravines and in all the settlements in the land. [14] I will tend them in a good pasture, and the mountain heights of Israel will be their grazing land... and there they will feed in a rich pasture on

the mountains of Israel. [15] I myself will tend my sheep and have them lie down, declares the Sovereign LORD. [16] I will search for the lost and bring back the strays. I will bind up the injured and strengthen the weak, but the sleek and the strong I will destroy. I will shepherd the flock with justice."

Based on the readings from John, Jeremiah, and Ezekiel in this chapter, please answer the following questions:

✓ *Questions For Individual Reflection Or Group Discussion:*

1. What are the different consequences to the sheep, community, land, and environment when either bad or good shepherds are in charge?

2. What are some of the qualities of bad and good shepherds?

3. How can we avoid being harmed by bad shepherds (or guard from becoming a "bad shepherd" ourselves) as we follow Christ and his call to care for each other and to "make disciples of all nations"?

4. Are we accountable for how we have cared for others? If so, how?

5. What are the consequences bad shepherds will endure?

6. What are the duties of the good shepherd as stipulated by Ezekiel in vs. 1-6 above?

7. How can we be good shepherds in our neighborhoods and churches? (Be specific)

8. Name at least 6 practical ways to be effective as Pastoral Care givers and good shepherds in today's complex world.

Case Study And Role Playing:

James and Jean have come to your church faithfully for the last 5 years and are members, but have quit coming entirely the last few months after a period of decreasing attendance. You have noticed some increasingly disturbing behavior from James in the last year as he has expressed dissatisfaction with the use of the NRSV scripture in the service and expressed belief that the KJ text is the only appropriate "real" version of the Bible. Jean used to be quite active on the Pastoral Care Team, but resigned 2 months ago after telling you that James felt it to be "inappropriate" and "unbiblical" for a woman to be in a position of leadership. Last night you received a disturbing phone call from Jean telling you she was frightened of James and the changes  she was seeing in him. Jean confessed to you that James had hit her after a recent argument and that another pastor had told her she should "submit to her husband." The other pastor told Jean that this violent action on James' part indicated she was not yet submissive enough to be a "true *Christian* woman." During your conversation on the phone with Jean, you have found out that James and Jean have been increasingly attending a large popular independent church in the area, where Pastor Dominion teaches that "women should remain silent in the church and submit to their husband in all things."

1. What will you do to provide Pastoral Care in this situation?

GROUP ACTIVITY

- ➢ *2. Make a comprehensive plan to provide pastoral care to all involved in this complex situation with others and/or your group.*

Chapter 4: Skills Needed For Pastoral Care: *Nuts And Bolts*

"Thy word O Lord is a lamp unto my feet and a light unto my path"
-Psalm 119:105

The skills needed for effective Pastoral Care are diverse, yet practical. All of these skills can be learned, although most people find themselves more naturally gifted in one area than another. Skills we will be learning more about include these vital areas of ongoing personal development:

P resence and prayerfulness

A vailability and Accountability

S ensitivity and self-knowledge

T oughness and tenderness

O rganization and Boundaries

R eliability and reasonableness

A sking the Right Questions

L ove, Hope, and Faith

C ompassionate Listening and Good Communications

A ppropriate Actions Biblically and Practically

R elationships that are Christ-Centered

E mpathy of a Healing Nature

GOOD COMMUNICATIONS

Good Communications are the core to all effective Pastoral Care. They are essential and consist of clarity, concern, and accuracy about what you are doing with both those that you are giving Pastoral Care to **and** those you are working with as members of a Ministry or Pastoral Care Team.

Inform your pastor and supervisors of what you are doing and who you are seeing. Be specific and prompt about any possible needs for follow-up care from the Senior Pastor or another member of your Pastoral Care Team. If you cannot talk directly to your team leader, a brief message should be left on the Senior Pastor's phone about anyone you have seen or talked to who is hospitalized, very ill, or in emotional or physical crisis.

Supervisors, Team Leaders, and Senior Pastors need to **be very specific** when requesting a team member engages in Pastoral Care on behalf of the ministry or church community. Accurate information should be given to the team member including: reasons for seeing the person, background, probable issues, what type of Pastoral Care is expected, and an initial estimate of approximately how many visits the care should extend to.

 **Accountability** is a vital part of good communications. When doing Pastoral Care, we are accountable to God, our Supervisor, Team Leader, and/or Senior Pastor, the Ministry Team support group, and ourselves. Ongoing Pastoral Care in the day and age we live in, with its overwhelming problems and complex demands, should not be attempted in isolation from a supportive Christian community or colleagues who can uphold and challenge us to keep growing and learning. Ministry Team **Support Groups** usually meet monthly for an hour or so in homes, the ministry office or church for review, support, and discussion of perceived Pastoral Care needs. Discussion of problematic visits or issues that have occurred in the church and larger community always need to be discussed. These *group meetings are confidential and supportive* and center on prayer, learning, and growth for all involved. They are based somewhat on John Wesley's model for the "Class Meeting" when the group began with the question of "How is it with the state of your soul?" Meetings should begin and end with prayers for wisdom and discernment.

Ongoing involvement in Pastoral Care certainly raises our own issues frequently, along with the issues of those we are ministering to. When dealing with issues of grief, crisis, loss, and trauma, we can become overwhelmed unless we have a safe place to discuss our own responses and feelings and look at different ways in which we can minister to others. This process always improves our abilities to give good Pastoral Care to others. But it also ensures we are not isolated but remain in a supportive loving community ourselves so we do not become "burned out" or "overwhelmed" by the needs of others. The rewards of Pastoral Care are enormous, but the demands can be just as enormous without proper support.

ORGANIZING MINISTRY AND PASTORAL CARE TEAMS

The way a church or ministry chooses to organize their ministry teams can be diverse. While structures need to be flexible, yet certain basics are essential for teams to be effective and work well for success and ministry continuity including provision for the six following vital areas:

1. A decision on the **name of your team** needs to be made. Some choose to call the group a Pastoral Care Team and others a "Ministry Team". However, it should have the name of your church or ministry included in the title to avoid confusion as to who or what your team represents.

2. A **regular monthly or bi-monthly meeting place and time** needs to be specified. Monthly meetings consist of communications about what each team member has been doing and who they have been seeing with a discussion as to actions that are working well and visits that don't seem to go as well. The group is there to offer support, suggestions, and additional resources. Assignments of particular care needs should be made to specific team members including all information available about the situation, person, family, problems, and needs.

3. **Appointment of a Team Coordinator** is needed of a gifted lay person to act as a coordinator between meetings. Their job is to co-ordinate communications with the team members, team leader, and senior pastor and notify members as to any changes in meeting times or places. The Coordinator will also inform team member of any changes in assignments, current crisis, emergencies, visitations needed, or practical needs, etc. This  assures the already busy Senior Pastor is not overloaded with administrative tasks and additional communications in their busy schedule but is always supported by team efforts.

4. Whenever possible it is recommended a **Team Consultant be appointed** with a degree and/or experience in aspects of either Mental Health, medical care, teaching, or Social Work, etc. that can be present for meetings and part or all of the training. Such individuals often already exist in many ministries and congregations who are also willing to volunteer their time. This can include either a Social Worker, Nurse, Counselor, Physician, Chaplain, or other appropriate people.

5. In order for a Pastoral Care Team to function at its optimum, a clear **Mission Statement needs to be adopted** after discussion and development. An eventual organizational pattern usually emerges that has a Leadership Team consisting of a gifted lay person to act as a Pastoral Care Team Coordinator, a Senior Pastor in charge, and usually a Consultant available for varying degrees of consultation regarding complex issues that can arise. Smaller churches and ministries tend to have one or two ministry teams that are more generalized in their mission. Larger churches may have numerous more specialized Ministry Teams focused on areas such as homelessness, crisis care, poverty, nursing homes, hunger, prisons, etc.

6. There needs to be willingness for each team member to agree to **adopt and adhere to a Team Ethical Code.** See an example of one in Appendix 3. This Mission Statement/Ethical Code has been used successfully for other pastoral care teams. Good Ethical Codes eliminate unneeded confusion, establish lines of authority, assure good organization and a consistent ethical manner of operating, and providing quality pastoral care that is organized and effective.

✓ Questions For Individual Reflection Or Group Discussion

1. What are your current goals for the Pastoral Care Team in your church?

2. What role do you hope it will play in the life of the church?

3. What role do you hope you will play in the Ministry Team?

4. What kinds of Pastoral Care visits do you feel comfortable with now?

5. What kinds of Pastoral Care visits would you like to have more discussion or training about?

6. How do you feel about being part of a Team Ministry support group?

7. When would be a good time to meet on a monthly basis for an hour for a Team meeting?

8. What official name would the group like to adopt for their own Team? (Be Specific)

GROUP ACTIVITY AND INDIVIDUAL ASSIGNMENT

Carefully read the Ethical Code/ Mission Statement in Appendix 2 for Ministry Teams and discuss it. Please discuss points you may find confusing and ask any questions that may prevent you from agreeing to this or a similar ethical code adopted by the Team. Develop a Mission Statement for your own team.

Chapter 5: Developing Pastoral Care Skills

There are probably no skills more important in the diverse areas of good Pastoral Care and effective Crisis Counseling than Listening, Prayer, and Good Communications. Concentration on developing abilities in these three areas can give anyone a sound foundation for all types of Pastoral Care.

PRAYER

John Wesley said "nothing happens without prayer." Those involved in the challenges and rewards of Pastoral Care soon find this absolutely true. Both silent and spoken prayers, along with private and public prayers, are vital for effective Pastoral Care. While we often worry about what is an "appropriate" prayer in Pastoral Care situations, the two models we can all use effectively in our own prayer life and Pastoral Care situations is the model used by Jesus in the Lord's Prayer and the model the writers of most of the Psalms offer. Jesus prayed from the heart directly to a personal caring and loving God and taught us to do the same. The writers of the Psalms also always speak from the heart with honesty and a forthrightness that is focused on the problem. Yet the psalmist is also comfortable with lamenting and naming deep feelings while still full of praise and thanksgiving to God for answering their prayers. The usual sequential model for prayer given in the psalms is usually one of:

- Praising or Honoring God;
- Naming the problem;
- Expressing honest feelings about the situation (including lament, grief, fear, anger, sadness, etc.);
- Acknowledging God's Power and provision for similar needs and situations in the past;
- Thanking God for answering the prayer and resolving the problems;
- Expressing Love for God and Praise of God - no matter what should befall.

These models for prayer given by Jesus or the one in the Psalms will not fail us in any situation needing prayer. If you are not comfortable praying spontaneously at this time in your life with other people, please study the Psalms for diverse prayers that can be used in different situations and then use them appropriately as your prayers by reading them in Pastoral Care situations. A small Bible is always appropriate to carry with you when engaged in Pastoral Care. **Before praying with another person, however, it is always important to ask if they would like**

prayer with a simple statement such as "Would you like me to pray about your situation now?" If the person indicates they are not open to verbal prayer, an appropriate response would be "I certainly understand. I want you to know that you and your loved ones will be in my heart and prayers in the days to come."

Pastoral Care visits should always be closed with prayer if the person if open to this possibility. This is a chance for the Holy Spirit ("Mighty Counselor") to minister through you as you pray with the person in need with honesty, empathy, sincerity, understanding, compassion, and love. Pray from the heart. Trust that the Holy Spirit will give you the words that are needed. Prayers do not have to be long to be effective. Brief, sincere, heartfelt prayers often minister most deeply to the wounded and hurting. The Lord's Prayer prayed together or separately is almost always appropriate if you have difficulty knowing what to pray.

LISTENING

Good Listening is an art that can be learned and a vital skill in giving effective Pastoral Care. Yet "accurate listening" is an area that may be very difficult for some of us. Our world and culture does not encourage good listening skills to develop. It is hard to hear ourselves or others or God in the continual noise that surrounds us in the modern world of cell phones, TV's, stereos, I-Pods, computers, jet planes, traffic, videos, radios, telephones, computers, etc.

Good Listening begins with *SILENCE*. In order to develop good listening skills, we first need to be comfortable in times of prayerful silence and learn to listen for God's still small voice in the presence of our own quiet devotional times. Only then can we learn to be present in a healing silence in the face of another person in need. It is in the discipline of silence that we learn to actively listen and accurately hear what the other person is really communicating.

One of the most effective types of supportive counseling is based on Dr. Carl Roger's work in "active listening." Active listening is hard work. It is other-centered and involves:

- Observation of appearance, dress, tone of voice, gestures, pauses, emotions manifested such as tears, laughter, etc.
- Your ability to repeat with some accuracy what the individual is saying.
- Manifesting empathetic, non-judgmental, relational approaches to others at all times.

It is often very difficult for hurting people to continue to talk with another person during a painful emotional time. You will need to develop the ability to repeat certain words to any distressed person that carried their most emotional tones in order to elicit further therapeutic sharing on their part. For instance, in the following conversation, you have observed that the specific words that are underlined convey the most emotions:

- *Pastoral Care Giver: How can I be of help?*
- Judy: I don't know. I feel so lost and afraid. I can't tell my husband the news. I keep thinking about my <u>mother</u>. (cries) I can't deal with the future, and I can't sleep. I feel paralyzed.
- *PCG: Mother?*
- Judy: Yes, she died of breast cancer. It was terrible. All that pain and chemotherapy and radiation. God, I can't go on! I feel so <u>abandoned</u>.
- *PCG: Abandoned?*
- Judy: Yes, it is terrible above all the feeling of emptiness and being <u>forsaken</u> and abandoned.
- *PCG: Forsaken?*
- Judy: You seem to really understand what I am saying and must know what it is like to be <u>hopeless</u>.

You can practice your "Active Listening Skills" in many situations that are not directly involved with Pastoral Care. Note how it changes the way others relate to you and how much deeper you are able to hear and understand others. Active listening does NOT involve talking about yourself unless it is therapeutically appropriate. With both prayer and listening skills in mind, the following case is offered to utilize all of your new learning to be most effective in a Pastoral Care situation.

Case Study And Group Role Playing

Judy has called you at 10PM and is quite distraught. She is apologetic for the late hour and says she needs someone to talk to and pray with her. You tell her that you would be glad to pray with her and ask if she would mind sharing what is "going on" so you can pray more effectively and be of better assistance. Judy reveals she has been to the doctor that afternoon and was told her latest mammogram revealed probable breast cancer that has most likely metastasized. She has been asked to come to the hospital for admission tomorrow morning for an immediate biopsy. Judy reveals, during the conversation, that her Mother died of breast cancer 10 years ago after a double mastectomy and a terrible ordeal of 5 years of pain, radiation, and chemotherapy. Judy says her husband and 2 daughters do not yet know of the mammogram finding indicating breast cancer. Judy says she feels both terrified and paralyzed. She is unable to sleep or tell the news to her husband and family.

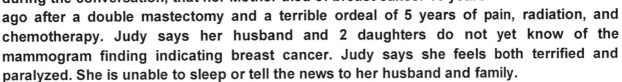

1. How will you minister to Judy using some of the training and information you have received so far? If possible, find a partner to role play with you. Each of you should take turns being "Judy" and the "Pastoral Care Giver."

2. Give each other feedback as to how you felt about the Pastoral Care given to you by your "partner."

GROUP ACTIVITY

> 3. *Discuss in the larger group what you learned from this particular Case Study experience and what worked and what did not.*

Chapter 6: Ensuring Effective Visits In Pastoral Care

While most people are apprehensive and somewhat anxious initially about being involved in pastoral care visits, attention to the following seven vital areas will ensure that the Pastoral Care you give is of the highest quality and as effective as possible.

1. PREPARE: Know or find out as much as possible about the "presenting problem" you are preparing to give Pastoral Care for. Pray for wisdom. Dress appropriately if this is face-to-face visit. Bare feet, short shirts, sagging pants, or plunging neck lines are not appropriate. Dress with respect for yourself and the other person. Take a small Bible with you, in case it is needed or appropriate for use. CALL AHEAD and arrange a mutually agreed on place and time to meet for a pastoral visit. If Pastoral Care visits involve hospitals, nursing home residents, or shut-ins, call ahead to find out visiting hours and any special needs. Some people may be comfortable with you coming to their home or the hospital, but others may not be. Respect their wishes. If you are meeting alone with a person of the opposite sex, it should be in a public place such as a mutually agreed on restaurant or coffee shop for the welfare of all concerned.

2. THE PASTORAL VISIT: The key to an effective pastoral visit is emotional availability and "presence" which can be defined as the conscious realization that you represent and convey the presence of the larger caring church community and the love of Christ to the person you are ministering to. You are not there to talk about yourself or to engage primarily in a social occasion, but are present to be an instrument of God's healing grace, compassion, and care. Listen carefully to the other person. Try to quietly ascertain the problems presented. Express understanding and empathy. Make a plan for any future actions you may wish to take, arrange for another meeting, if necessary, and pray before you end the visit. ***Remember always that all Pastoral Care is CONFIDENTIAL unless there is a "need to know." Your Senior Pastor and/or supervisor/consultant always have a "need to know." Any important information or crisis concerns should be shared with them ASAP by leaving a phone answering machine message or cell phone contact in emergencies. The Senior Pastor and/or Team Leader should be told immediately of suicide threats or reports of abuse.***

3. ETHICAL CODES are essential to the establishment and maintenance of effective Pastoral Care Teams. Adherence to the highest **ethical codes** for Pastoral Care are essential for: your welfare, to assure the best possible care for those you are seeing, the protection of your church and pastor, and the furtherance of the mission of the Pastoral Care Team. Please review carefully the ethical code in Appendix 3 for Pastoral Care Teams and their members. The motto and purpose of a good ethical code is: "Take care of your ethical code, and it will take care of you!"

4. MISSION STATEMENTS and knowing clearly the meaning and intent of your mission and purpose in your Ministry Team is essential for success. People have different gifts within the context of Pastoral Care. One may love to send cards; another thrives on home visits but avoids hospital visits. Yet another person may despise home visits and thrive on hospital or emergency care visits. Another may love repairing homes or feeding the hungry. ALL are needed, and no one

is expected to excel in all aspects of Pastoral Care. Working TOGETHER, we become the hands and heart of Christ providing care for the flock. The Ministry Team, in time and with prayer, will reflect the body of Christ and bring its light and healing presence to those struggling in grief and walking a dark path. While mission statements of various ministries or churches may vary somewhat, the principles of the Mission statement in Appendix 3 for Pastoral Care Teams may be used as a basis. Or your ministry can develop their own variations of this basic mission statement. It is dangerous and confusing for all concerned to try to function as a Pastoral Care Team without a specific mission statement and a comprehensive ethical code that is clearly understood by all involved.

5. BOUNDARIES in ending visits by Ministry Team members are crucial. Hospital visits or those to the sick should be short in order not to tire the patient. 15 minutes is the max for the acutely ill unless they are dying and the family has asked that you be present during this time. For shut-ins and nursing home residents who are lonely and frequently isolated, 30 minutes to an hour is acceptable. More time can be exhausting for all concerned. Home visits and external Pastoral Care visits in restaurants or coffee shops should not exceed an hour, except in unusual circumstances as the occasion can become a social one and draining to those concerned.

6. REFERRALS are vital in good Pastoral Care. Know the resources available in your community. Your local United Way office or Mental Health Center usually keeps a free list or booklet of agencies that provide specialized care in counseling, crisis lines, emergency assistance and shelter, etc. This booklet can be presented as resource possibilities to those you are providing Pastoral Care for, when appropriate. Always make it clear that the use of such resources is up to the individual concerned, and that you are offering it as "possibilities that may be helpful." A comprehensive form for organizing local phone numbers in pastoral or crisis care is provided in Appendix 2. Every team member should have a copy with the addresses and phone numbers filled in for your local situation.

7. REFLECTION: As you are reflect on your visit, it may be helpful to jot down a few notes after you leave. Never write your personal care notes in the presence of the person you are caring for! A brief "Pastoral Visit Form" similar to the one in Appendix 1, or something close to it, should be filled out at least monthly. This type of Form can be very useful for learning, growth, keeping track of what you are doing, and maintaining useful records. It works well for accountability, effective communication with your pastor, consultant, or support group, and case conference presentations of your work, and future planning at Pastoral Care Team support group meetings. Comprehensive or expanded "treatment plans" for those you are caring for will emerge as you consult with others in your team, coordinate your efforts with the Leaders, and bring complex or difficult case situations to the attention of the monthly support group.

✓ *Questions For Individual Reflection Or Group Discussion*

1. Which of the seven areas discussed in this chapter do you feel most competent in? Which areas do you struggle with most?

2. What specific information discussed have you found most useful so far?

3. What other areas in Pastoral Care would you like to see addressed in the future?

4. What previous experiences have you had in caring for others?

GROUP ACTIVITIES

1. Discuss as a group the resources offered in Appendix 1, 2, and 3. These resources have been developed and used effectively by other Ministry Teams and are offered as an example of what tools you will need for success as a Ministry Team. They are examples that can provide suggestions and a starting point for partial use as your own Team develops. Similar tools will be necessary for your own Team to ensure smooth functioning and protection of all concerned.

2. If you wish to do so, how could you adapt these resources to your local situation?

3. Assign someone to complete the phone numbers and addresses in Appendix 2 in order to have them available for your Ministry Team's use or do so as a group project. Appendix 2 is not meant to imply these are <u>ALL</u> the numbers you may want to include, but does contain many of those generally used.

4. As a group, if you have not done so yet, Create your own Mission Statement and Ethical code either by adapting the principles of the ones presented in Appendix 3 to your local needs or using other Ethical Codes of equal value.

5. Discuss the use of the "Pastoral Visit" Form in Appendix 1. This is a brief form designed to be filled out in a few minutes after visits to ensure successful care. Something similar is necessary to maintain vital but minimal info necessary for good care and accountability. Discuss any questions or concerns in group you may have about the use of a similar tool. Decide what method or tool your team wants to use for this purpose.

MEDITATION

"There are different kinds of gifts, but the same Spirit. [5] There are different kinds of service, but the same Lord. [6] There are different kinds of working, but the same God works all of them in all men. [7] Now to each one the manifestation of the Spirit is given for the common good. [8] To one there is given through the Spirit the message of wisdom, to another the message of knowledge by means of the same Spirit, [9] to another faith by the same Spirit, to another gifts of healing by that one Spirit, [10] to another miraculous powers, to another prophecy, to another distinguishing between spirits, to another speaking in different kinds of tongues, and to still another the interpretation of tongues. [11] All these are the work of one and the same Spirit, and he gives them to each one, just as he determines.

[12] The body is a unit, though it is made up of many parts; and though all its parts are many, they form one body. So it is with Christ. [13] For we were all baptized by one Spirit into one body--whether Jews or Greeks, slave or free--and we were all given the one Spirit to drink. [14] Now the body is not made up of one part but of many. [15] If the foot should say, "Because I am not a hand, I do not belong to the body," it would not for that reason cease

Pastoral Care only happens when we "choose" to care, not when we wait until we are problem free. Caring always involves courage. Even while Paul was in prison, he chose to care and provide Pastoral Care for others despite his own difficulties. Our own struggles are not obstacles to care, but in reality they equip us to give compassionate care.

Our willingness to sacrifice a degree of freedom or "free time" is often at the heart of Pastoral Care. Hebrews 4:16 reminds us: "Let us then approach the throne of grace with confidence, so that we may receive mercy and find grace to help us in our time of need."

If we become unsure, confused, or afraid in demanding Pastoral Care situations, we need to remember that we are never alone for Jesus said; *"All this I have spoken while still with you. But the Counselor, the Holy Spirit, whom the Father will send in my name, will teach you all things and will remind you of everything I have said to you. Peace I leave with you; my peace I give you. I do not give to you as the world gives. Do not let your hearts be troubled and do not be afraid." (John 14:25-27)*

to be part of the body. [16] And if the ear should say, "Because I am not an eye, I do not belong to the body," it would not for that reason cease to be part of the body. [17] If the whole body were an eye, where would the sense of hearing be? If the whole body were an ear, where would the sense of smell be?

[18] But in fact God has arranged the parts in the body, every one of them, just as he wanted them to be. [19] If they were all one part, where would the body be? [20] As it is, there are many parts, but one body. [21] The eye cannot say to the hand, "I don't need you!" And the head cannot say to the feet, "I don't need you!" [22] On the contrary, those parts of the body that seem to be weaker are indispensable, [23] and the parts that we think are less honorable we treat with special honor. And the parts that are unpresentable are treated with special modesty, [24] while our presentable parts need no special treatment. But God has combined the members of the body and has given greater honor to the parts that lacked it, [25] so that there should be no division in the body, but that its parts should have equal concern for each other. [26] If one part suffers, every part suffers with it; if one part is honored, every part rejoices with it. [27] Now you are the body of Christ, and each one of you is a part of it." (1 Corinthians 12:4-28; NIV)

✓ Questions For Individual Reflection Or Group Discussion

1. What does it mean personally to be part of the "body of Christ" for you?

2. How have your own struggles equipped you to give better pastoral care?

3. Write a brief general prayer to be used at the end of a pastoral visit.

APPENDIX 1
Visitation Form

Name _____   Ministry _____   Time Period _____

Person Visited	Type of Visit	Date	Action Taken	Follow-up Needed?	Informed Pastor?	Issues

APPENDIX 2
Crisis Resource Phone Numbers/Addresses

Emergency Room_____

Ambulance_____

Church/Ministry_____

Senior Pastor_____

Team Coordinator_____

Team Consultant_____

Police_____

Homeless Shelter_____

Women's Shelter _____

Suicide Hotline_____

Housing Assistance_____

Legal Aid_____

Food Pantries_____

Mental Health Services_____

Catholic Charities_____

Red Cross_____

Salvation Army_____

United Way_____

Town/City Clerk_____

Domestic Violence Hotline_____

Pastoral Counseling Center_____

Community Kitchen_____

APPENDIX 3

Mission Statement Of Our Ministry Team (Example)

Our Ministry Team exists to "bring Good News to the poor and heal the brokenhearted." (Lk. 4:18) We will do so by augmenting the Pastoral Care Outreach of our church both within the congregation and surrounding communities by visitation, crisis care, appropriate practical assistance, intercessory prayer, cooperation with the Pastoral Care efforts of the Pastor and other team members, and support of the pastor. We commit ourselves to work respectfully together as a team so that the best possible care is given to those in need of Pastoral and Crisis Care. We pledge ourselves to work cooperatively together with mutual respect and appreciation and to provide the finest quality care possible while adhering to the highest ethics involving confidentiality of those cared for and accountability to our ministry. In support of our mission, we promise to faithfully adhere to the following:

Ethical Code For Pastoral Care Teams (Example)

1) Team Members will deal truthfully with each other and those we care for and encourage free and open discussion while upholding the best interests, rights, and well-being of all concerned. We will respect and honor the leadership of the Senior Pastor's guidance and direction.

2) We will respect the right of all people to privacy and confidentiality of information except when there is a clear and imminent danger to self or others, at which time we will immediately inform the proper authorities after proper consultation with the Senior Pastor and Team Leadership. We will avoid gossip at all times.

3) In order to assure the best Pastoral Care is given to all, we will use individual gifts and abilities given to us wisely while communicating necessary information to other team members about any and all cases assigned to us. We will stay informed of any new Pastoral Care situations by participating on a regular basis in monthly case presentations at Pastoral Care Team meetings. We will remain accountable to the Senior Pastor and Ministry Team, so that we can profit by the support and wisdom of the group support case conference. This will be organized by the Coordinator and led either by the Senior Pastor or officially designated consultants who have specialized training in Pastoral Care. We will follow-up on redirection and suggestions from the case support group when appropriate to improve Pastoral Care we are providing.

4) We will exercise due caution when communicating through the Internet, other electronic means, and verbally outside of a Team meeting in order to respect the privacy and confidentiality of those we are providing Pastoral Care for. When presenting cases in our monthly Ministry Team meetings, we will not use real names in order to protect privacy.

5) We will respect each other and support the integrity and well-being of our colleagues and team members with prayer, accountability, honesty, sensitivity and mutual co-operation. In case of concerns or disagreements, we agree to adhere to the best Christian principles of conflict resolution as contained in Matthew 18 and to resolve misunderstandings and concerns within the context of the lines of authority within the Pastoral Care Team organization by contacting the Coordinator, Pastor, and current Consultant with issues and concerns not resolved in group case discussion.

6) We will take collegial and responsible action when concerns arise about, or we have direct knowledge of: incompetence, impairment, misconduct, or violations against this code. We will share such concerns, if they arise, with the Pastor, Team Coordinator, and current Consultant who, together, will meet privately with the Team member(s) in order to address such sensitive issues, rather than discussing potentially embarrassing or divisive matters in the group meetings or case conferences. Members who manifest repeated or serious violations of the Ethical Code may be respectfully asked to resign from Team membership with the recommendations of the Team Coordinator, Consultant, and Senior Pastor.

7) We will respect the right of people to privacy and confidentiality of information except when there is a clear and imminent danger to those people or others; at which time they will be informed of those limits of confidentiality. We will recognize the dignity and worth of every person and will offer Pastoral Care without unfair discrimination.

8) We will not abuse our position by taking advantage of people for personal, financial or institutional gain and recognize that physical intimacy in a Pastoral Care situation or even the appearance of impropriety is unacceptable and could compromise our Christian witness. Therefore, we will avoid potentially compromising situations while being sensitive to needs for privacy in Pastoral Care situations.

9) We will recognize that there are limits to our competence as a Pastoral Care Team member and will refer people appropriately to others better qualified when this proves necessary or desirable after discussion with the Senior Pastor and/or after a case conference presentation. We will not attempt formal counseling without proper training.

10) We will recognize there are proper contexts and methods for Pastoral Care and will act with awareness and sensitivity to this reality and will use regular approved supervision and/or consultation at case conferences to maintain accountability and a high standard of Pastoral Care.

11) We will take advantage of opportunities for personal spiritual growth when possible and seek to enhance our knowledge and skill in the areas of Pastoral and Crisis Care by continuing education when available and as needed.

THOUGHTS FOR CONTEMPLATION

"To be is better than to do. The same wind that uproots a tree lifts a bird. What happens in us is more important than what happens to us. When we stand before God, He will not ask us if we have been successful, but if we have been faithful" -Anonymous

"Do all the good you can, by all the means you can, in all the ways you can, in all the places you can, at all the times you can, to all the people you can, as long as ever you can." -John Wesley

"Before you speak, it is necessary for you to listen, for God speaks in the silence of the heart." -Mother Theresa

"Never believe that a few caring people can't change the world. For, indeed, that's all who ever have." -Margaret Mead

"God's dream is that you and I and all of us will realize that we are family, that we are made for togetherness, for goodness, and for compassion." -Desmond Tutu

"Let there be kindness in your face, in your eyes, in your smile, in the warmth of your greeting. Always have a cheerful smile. Don't only give your care, but give your heart as well." -Mother Theresa

Activating The Power Of Pastoral Care
A TEAM APPROACH

PART 2

CRISIS CARE

THE ART AND SKILLS OF CRISIS COUNSELING

By

Rev. Dr. Mary B. Johnson

"But the Counselor, the Holy Spirit, whom the Father will send in my name, will teach you all things...... I do not give as the world gives. Do not let your hearts be troubled and do not be afraid." -Jesus (Jn.14:25)

Introduction: **CRISIS CARE**

Art and Skills of Christian Crisis Counseling

OUR AGE OF CRISIS

We live in an age of continuing Crisis. From the alarmist morning news to the cataclysmic evening news, we are assaulted by the latest instant continuing electronic coverage of earthquakes, murders, terrorist attacks, red alerts, war casualties, riots, assaults, homicides, economic disasters, mass murder, plagues, floods, hurricanes, tornadoes, and the consequences of spreading global warming. Contents of the evening newspaper often appear more and more like an inserted page from the Book of Revelation. Concurrently, crisis seems to shadow our own lives as stress continues to mount in a society that is watching the disappearance of the extended family, weakening of the nuclear family, dissolution of traditional values, and emergence of "alternative" lifestyles as the increasing norm. Consequently, many of our familiar support systems such as family, home, friends, and church communities seem to be weakening in the assaults around us as change accelerates. Inevitably personal crisis comes to us all.

The overwhelming problem we now face both personally and as a society is that we no longer have the traditional support systems in place to nurture us through the inevitable crises around us to times of new beginnings of recovery and healing. Pastors, mental health workers, and doctors are no longer able to "do it all" alone as the grave toll of unmet needs for crisis care continues to impact on our citizens, society, and churches. Inadequate and improper care in crisis situations can lead to a host of continuing problems including, poverty, post traumatic stress disorder, depression, suicide, anxiety disorders, psychosis, addictions, bitterness, loss of faith, isolation, violence, chronic mental and physical illness, isolation, and despair. Many Types of Counseling exist including:

- Individual,
- Marital,
- Family,
- Group,
- Assessment & Diagnosis,
- Addiction,
- Supportive,
- Educational.
- Crisis.

However, Crisis Care/Counseling is unique in the manifold opportunities for healing and community outreach presented by crisis. It is necessary as a vital part of Pastoral Care and needed in all of our churches and diverse communities. Religious Communities are usually called In Crisis. Yet the question remains *"Will We Be Ready To Serve As Healing Agents In Our Communities"?* The *Archives Of Family Medicine (1998; Nov.-Dec.)* reported the following:

○ **More than 80% of the physicians reported they refer or recommend their patients to clergy and pastoral care providers;** more than 30% stated that they refer more than 10 times a year.

○ Many physicians (75.5%) chose conditions associated with crisis or end-of-life care (Bereavement, Terminal Illness) as reasons for referral. Marital and family counseling were cited by 72.8% of physicians. Other issues for referral included Depression and Mood Disorders (38.7%) and Substance Abuse (19.0%).

○ Most family physicians seek and accept clergy and pastoral professionals in the care of their patients. **In medical settings, the providers of religious and spiritual interventions have a larger role than previously reported.**

 While the term "Counseling" can be frightening when used on a formal basis, every person will eventually be called upon to use counseling skills when asked to stand with those in need suffering a crisis. We should ALL be prepared to offer good Crisis Care in times of emergency and acute stress. We need to remember that Jesus commissioned his followers to CARE and heal the sick as part of the proclamation of the Good News. Christian disciples are expected to be engaged in active caring healing ministries. Luke the physician tells us, *"When Jesus had called the Twelve together, he gave them power and authority to drive out all demons and to cure diseases, and he sent them out to preach the kingdom of God and to* ***heal*** *the sick." (Lk.9:1-2).* Our challenge today is to find ways in which we too as a church in the modern world can reach out with healing hands in our communities. Some ways may include:

- Offering church facilities for crisis *support groups* in the areas of grief, health issues, etc. Consider making space available for Recovery Groups like AA (Alcoholics Anonymous), NA (Narcotics Anonymous), or support groups for families in stress.
- Establishing a *"Crisis Care Ministry Team"* in your church. Demands for crisis support and pastoral care in our troubled society are too great for any one person or lone pastor to meet by themselves.
- Form a pastoral *"Healing Ministry Team"* to pray and minister together with anyone seeking healing from trauma, sickness, or stress. A team is more effective than solo efforts. Jesus sent disciples out in pairs for good reason. Utilize proven Christian ancient practices of *anointing with oil and laying on of hands* when praying for healing. These practices are discussed in the New Testament extensively.

Chapter 7: **Crisis, Stress, And Crisis Counseling**

Relationship of Stress to Crisis

Experts in the scientific community are continually learning about the stress caused by acute and continuing crisis and its consequent related illness. Unresolved crisis leads to chronic stress which seems to be a contributing factor to everything from cancer and chronic fatigue syndrome to backaches and insomnia. Stress impacts health by lowering our resistance to disease and making us more vulnerable to illness.

Our body responds to emotional stress the same way it reacts to physical danger. When we feel the effects of stress, our health is compromised by a primitive fight or flight response that produces stress hormones even when we are not really in immediate danger. Each day, crisis situations that cause stress affect our health by making us prone to illness, heart attacks, disease, and making us age more rapidly. Stress, which research has related to a variety of illness and diseases, becomes toxic to our overall health when we process stress as a negative factor and let it continually eat us up on an emotional level.

To ease stress and improve our chances of avoiding stress related illness, it seems important to not "push ourselves so hard", physicians warn us. We are advised to avoid negative thinking and choose our battles carefully while letting the little things slide instead of boiling over with anger. Our health will improve we are told with these simple measures, and we will notice feeling less fatigued, irritable, and uptight. Health professionals warn us to not let the effects of stress and crisis rule us in a negative way and impact us by diminishing our much needed supportive networks of family, friendships, community, church, and other important relationships. Statistics back up the theory of stress related illness tied to unresolved or continuing crisis. In fact, stress accounts for two-thirds of family doctor visits and half the deaths to Americans under the age of 65 according to the U.S. Centers for Disease Control and Prevention. If you have a stomach, heart, or mental disorder, your doctor may have attributed

STRESS & CRISIS

Responsible For 66% of All Doctor's Visits

Related To 75% of All Illness

your condition to stress. Stress is also related to headaches, backaches, cholesterol, and high blood pressure. Studies by the American Medical Association have also shown the negative effects of stress on health. They say stress is a factor in more than 75 percent of all illness and disease today. The negative effects of stress on health are indisputable. Interestingly enough, stress has been the subject of more than 20,000 scientific studies.

One 10-year study by Kiecolt-Glaser looked at the effects of stress on illness of medical students. The researchers found decreased levels of the body's natural killer cells, which fight infections and tumors, during even the familiar stress periods of exams. Whether you are studying for a test or just trying to pay the family bills, stress can have an irreversible negative effect on health. Another study published in *"Circulation: Journal of the American Heart Association"* showed how mental stress can decrease blood flow to the heart. Studies on stress related illness equated stress with cholesterol and smoking as risk factors in heart disease. Even though studies confirm stress has devastating consequences for our overall heath, Americans often pride themselves on working even longer and harder, staying on top of the competition, and working more. To break free from the vicious stress cycle and stave off illness, disease, emotional fatigue, and depression, we are encouraged to try relaxation techniques and are told our overall health will improve if we get plenty of rest. Exercise, eating right, and avoiding drugs and caffeine are known ways to help heal our bodies of the negative effects of unresolved crisis and stress on our overall health. However, a purely secular approach to crisis counseling and stress management is unfortunately limited in addressing the complex underlying issues and is usually focused on the body to the exclusion of spirit, soul, and community.

Holistic Approaches to Crisis Care

Without addressing the **whole** person and the societal context underlying our crisis prone world, secular measures in Crisis Care and Stress reduction are merely temporary. Crisis Counseling cannot be truly effective without a clear understanding of the whole nature of the human person. Approaches that only address the physical aspect of our nature are doomed to failure. Ancient societies, such as the New Testament Hellenistic or Greek culture, had a far better understanding of the complexity of our

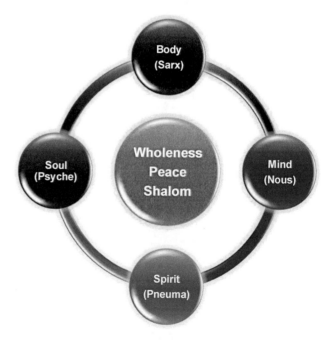

humanity and understood us to be composed of: body (*sarx*), mind (*nous*), soul (*psyche*), and spirit (*pneuma*). The ancient Hebrew understanding of "healing" was rooted in the biblical concept of "shalom" or "wholeness" which involved a harmony of body, mind, spirit, and soul in right relationship with the Creation and the Creator. Whatever things disrupted that harmonious world wholeness and balance was looked on as "dis-ease" producing and causing one to "miss the mark" or be affected by "sin" which literally means "miss the mark" in Hebrew. This state is viewed as affecting our sense of connection with God and a right relationship with self and neighbor. In order for a person to "heal', both harmony and balance must be restored internally with one's own self but also externally with God, neighbor, and the environment.

Biblically, Crisis was seen as a force that could disrupt and shatter God's intended balance and harmony dissolving "shalom" or "peace". It is in this context that Jesus spoke to his disciples about the critical importance of Counseling in crisis as he was approaching his own death by crucifixion when he said, *"All this I have spoken while still with you. But the **Counselor**, the Holy Spirit, whom the Father will send in my name, will teach you all things and will remind you of everything I have said to you. Peace I leave with you; my peace I give you. I do not give to you as the world gives. Do not let your hearts be troubled and do not be afraid."* (Jn. 14:25-27; NIV) *"If you love me, you will obey what I command. And I will ask the Father, and he will give you another Counselor to be with you forever - the Spirit of truth. The world cannot accept him, because it neither sees him nor knows him. But you know him, for he lives with you and will be in you. I will not leave you as orphans; I will come to you. Before long, the world will not see me anymore, but you will see me. Because I live, you also will live.* (Jn. 14:15-19; NIV)

✓ *Questions For Individual Reflection Or Group Discussion*

1. In light of the information presented so far, how do you feel a Christian approach to healing is different from a secular approach?

2. What ways are chronic stress and unresolved crisis affecting your life and the lives of those you know?

3. What do you think Jesus meant when he said, in the passage above from John, that he would send us a "Counselor"?

4. What implications does this have for your life and ministry?

5. What implications does this have for the ministry and mission of your church?

CASE STUDY

Marie had a conversation with you after church at Fellowship Time in which she seemed very upset and teary eyed. You asked her if she was all right, and she responded "NO" and started weeping profusely. You asked her if she would like to talk more in a less crowded place and took her to one of the empty Sunday school rooms and told her you would be glad to listen if that would be of help. Subsequently, Marie revealed that her husband Juan had been arrested by immigration officials yesterday and would most likely be deported for not having a green card. She stated while weeping profusely that there is

 not enough food in the house to feed her five children for another day. She also said she cannot sleep and feels frightened and hopeless and cannot stop crying. Marie also expressed deep concern about the Christmas holiday in two weeks and showed great grief about the fact she can't afford any Christmas gifts for her children. She stated she cannot cope and life seems "not worth living without Juan."

1. How will you offer Holistic Crisis Care in this situation and address Body, Mind, Soul, Spirit, and Community in a healing way?

GROUP ACTIVITY

➢ *2. What will be your treatment plan for Marie as a group acting as a Ministry Team?*

Chapter 8: Interventions In Crisis

Intervention

Appropriate Crisis Counseling is essential in times of Crisis, when our peace, harmony, and wholeness is shattered by intervening dark forces of chaos that can separate us from a harmonious relationship with God and ourselves. Causes of acute crises can include: physical illness, loss of loved ones, grief, sorrow, divorce, tragedy, poverty, war, violence, injury, assault, evil, enemy attack, shame, persecution, prison, rape, molestation, etc. This leads to a vicious self-perpetuating cycle generating unending crisis resulting in a damaging "permanent stress" *unless* intervention is made to restore wholeness or healing. Therefore, Jesus says that a redemptive intervening force that brings a "Spirit of Truth" ("Mighty Counselor") is needed to bring life and healing and restore Balance, Harmony, Wholeness, and "Shalom" or Peace.

In order to accomplish healing from the shattering results of Crisis, we need an Advocate, Counselor, Redeemer, Messiah (or "anointed one" in Hebrew), Good Shepherd, or the "Holy Spirit" to **Intervene** and remold us and rectify the internal and external brokenness that Crisis produces in our lives. Or as the prophet Isaiah predicted of the Messiah: *"Surely he took up our infirmities and carried our sorrows, yet we considered him stricken by God, smitten by him, and afflicted. But he was pierced for our transgressions, he was crushed for our iniquities; the punishment that brought us peace was upon him, and by his wounds we are healed." (Isaiah 53:4-5)*

Intervention distinguishes Crisis Care from other types of pastoral care and counseling. Intervention is called for in crises to establish order, safety, security, and make avenues for healing. *Action* distinguishes Crisis Care from the supportive kinds of listening predominant in chronic situations requiring classical pastoral care. If appropriate intervention is made in a timely manner at the point of the crisis, then the resultant vicious cycle of stress, anxiety, despair, and sickness leading to more Crises can usually be avoided. In order to be effective, Interventions must be focused on the acute problem, appropriate, timely, and mutually agreed to by both the person in crisis

and the Crisis Care Giver. Interventions are problem oriented and focus on practical tangible solutions to acute needs. If you do not have the resources available to meet such needs through your church community, then appropriate referrals to community resources are a vital part of appropriate interventions and become critical to good Crisis Care.

It is within this context and biblical understanding that we can all begin to have a better grasp of how we too can function most effectively as effective "Crisis Care Givers" in our troubled world and communities, no matter what our background is or what the specific problem is. Effective productive **Biblical Crisis Counseling** is based on the scriptural model of Jesus as Healer and *Advocate*. We are called to be Advocates for those in crisis if we follow the biblical model of crisis care and the example and teachings of Jesus. If we follow the great commission of Jesus to "go into all the world and proclaim the Good News and as you go teach, preach, heal, and cast out demons", then we will find the healing promises of Jesus are true. Indeed, he will send each of us another "Counselor", even the Holy Spirit or "Spirit of Truth", to walk beside us and reside in us with the wisdom and strength equal to the task of bringing healing to the afflicted in the midst of crisis and chaos. No matter the nature of the diverse crises that may face us and those we care for, the basic procedures for all Crisis Counseling is the same. While knowledge of specific types of crisis such as bereavement, grief, addiction, divorce, abuse, domestic violence, etc. is helpful in Crisis Counseling, the overall principles and procedures are the same in any type of crisis counseling.

CRISIS COUNSELING or CRISIS CARE, in order to be effective, always calls for us to respond to crisis situations with:

Compassion,

Respect,

Intervention,

Support,

Instruction

Spiritual Sensitivity.

Remembering this acronym for the **CRISIS** care we are called to give in all **CRISIS**

SITUATIONS requiring our attention, will ensure that any counseling also offered will be effective. We need to be focused on healing with the goal of eventually intervening appropriately in the Crisis. Our purpose is to re-establish wholeness and bring "peace" or healing which is called "Shalom" in the Hebrew understanding and language.

✓ Questions For Individual Reflection Or Group Discussion

1. What kind of crisis situations have you been in where others ministered to you effectively?

2. What did you find most helpful?

3. What was not helpful?

4. What distinguishes "crisis care" from classical "pastoral care"? How are they different?

CASE STUDY

It is midnight in January and George and Kay have just called you from their cell phone to let you know that they are outside their home with the police due to a fire that is causing extensive damage. When John hands the phone to Kay she starts crying and says that although their three children are safe with them, that the beloved family dog is trapped inside their burning home. Kay shares with you that it appears the house will be a total loss and she wonders if you, or the church community, can assist their family. The family has been a vital part of the church community for over 10 years. Kay is a Sunday school teacher, and George is active in the choir.

1. What is your overall treatment plan?

GROUP ACTIVITY

> *2. What will you do as a group or Ministry Team to make an appropriate and timely intervention in order to give good crisis care in this situation?*

Chapter 9: **Developing Crisis Counseling Skills**

COUNSELING is an ancient art discussed at length in the Bible which contains many references to the necessity of godly counselors and the basis for good counseling. Scriptural references abound such as:

"The counsel of the LORD stands forever, the plans of His heart to all generations." (Psalms 33:11; NKJV)

"You, Lord, will guide me with your counsel, and afterward receive me to glory. Whom have I in heaven but You? And there is none upon earth that I desire besides you. My flesh and my heart fail; but God is the strength of my heart and my portion forever. (Psalms 73:24-26; NKJV)

"A wise man will hear and increase learning, and a man of understanding will attain wise counsel," (Prov. 1:5; NKJV)

"....And in a multitude of counselors there is safety." (Prov. 24:6; NKJV)

"Without counsel purposes are disappointed: but in the multitude of counselors they are established. A man hath joy by the answer of his mouth and a word spoken in due season, how good is it!" (Prov. 15:22-23; KJV)

"I am God, and there is none like Me, declaring the end from the beginning, and from ancient times things that are not yet done, saying, 'My counsel shall stand, " (Isaiah 46:9-10; NKJV)

"For unto us a child is born, to us a son is given; and the government shall be upon his shoulder, and his name shall be called Wonderful Counselor, Mighty God, Everlasting Father, Prince of Peace. Of the increase of his government and of peace there will be no end," (Isaiah 9:6-7; ESV)

COUNSELING BASICS IN CRISIS CARE

The Bible clearly shows us that there can be no effective *COUNSELING* without three essential basic elements which involve: a trusting **Relationship**, **Wisdom,** and **Caring.** The Bible also uses words such as "Comfort", "Care, "Compassion", "Wisdom", "Guidance", etc. for "Counseling". However, we live a modern litigatious age where the mention of the word "counseling" is unfortunately too often equated legally with "psychotherapy". Since the very term "counseling" is sometimes relegated by law in some states to the exclusive use of those who are state licensed professionals, it is wise to be cautious in claiming to be doing "counseling" *per se* in our legalistic society and refer to involvement with healing and pastoral care outreach as "Crisis Care". Often the term "Life Coaching" is used for activities that the Bible refers to as counseling. However, the use of varied terminologies does *no*t negate the fact that the use and knowledge of vital basic counseling skills are essential to doing effective crisis care or pastoral care.

RELATIONSHIP OF TRUST

The presence of a **Relationship of Trust** and respect is critical for any kind of effective crisis counseling or crisis care to be effective. This principal is beautifully portrayed in the story of Jesus healing the woman with the hemorrhage (see Mark 5:25-34). She has the faith or "trust" to touch

Christ in spite of her "unclean" condition under the Law. Even knowing she could be severely punished for such an action, she continued to desperately press through the crowds, convinced that if only she could touch the hem of the garment of the Rabbi from Nazareth she would be healed. In response to this incredible act of trust, Jesus says *"Woman, go in Peace!" Your Faith has made you well. Be healed of your disease."* When we understand that the definition of faith is "trust" this story comes alive and we then realize that a **RELATIONSHIP OF TRUST,** or Faith, is necessary for healing. Without it, wholeness cannot occur. A trusting relationship is crucial to any healing. How we establish the Trust of another in us, as we offer counseling in crisis situations, will be discussed later in detail.

WISDOM

Another vital part of effective counseling in crisis care is **WISDOM**. Wisdom is referred to as "*Sophia*" in Hebrew and is female in grammatical tense, as is "Spirit", which wisdom is closely affiliated with. When Jesus referred to the Holy Spirit in his native language, "Spirit" would have been understood to be female. When translated into the Greek of the New Testament, "Spirit" became male in grammatical tense. The healing presence of **WISDOM** in our counseling is beautifully described at length in Proverbs where it is stated, *"Does not wisdom cry out, and* *understanding lift up her voice? She takes her stand on the top of the high hill, beside the way, where the paths meet. She cries out by the gates, at the entry of the city, at the entrance of the doors: "To you, O men, I call, and my voice is to the sons of men.....The fear of the LORD is to hate evil; pride and arrogance and the evil way and the perverse mouth I hate.* **Counsel** *is mine, and sound wisdom; I understand, I have strength. (Prov. 8:1-14; NKJV)*

CARING

The necessity of **CARING** to bring forth harmony, healing, and peace as fruits of our crisis care and counseling is beautifully described in the written counsel of Paul the Apostle to the members of the church in Corinth when he writes, *"For just as the body is one and has many members, and all the members of the body, though many are one body, so it is with Christ. [13] For in one Spirit we were all baptized into one body - Jews or Greeks, slaves or free - and all were made to drink of one Spirit. [14] For the body does not consist of one member but of many...But God has so composed the body, giving greater honor to the part that lacked it, [25] that there may be no division in the body, but that the members may have the same* **_care_** *for one another. [26] If one member suffers, all suffer together; if one member is honored, all rejoice together. [27] Now you are the body of Christ and individually members of it. [28] And God has appointed in the church first apostles, second prophets, third teachers, then miracles, then gifts of healing, helping, administrating, and various kinds of tongues." (1 Cor. 12:12-29; ESV)*

SPECIFIC COUNSELING SKILLS

While many types of Counseling exist including Individual, Marital, Family, Group, Assessment, Addiction, Supportive, and Educational, it seems the manifold opportunities for healing presented by the necessity of Crisis Care are unique. **Crisis Pastoral Care** is needed in all of our religious communities and churches. It is the pastor, pastoral care team, and members of the religious community that are most often contacted first for help in times of death, bereavement, acute illness, loss, marital and family problems, depression, fear, critical needs, birth, acute poverty, trauma, loneliness, etc.

C-Compassion
R-Respect
I-Intervention
S-Support
I-Instruction
S-Spiritual Focus

CRISIS COUNSELING

C-Concern
O-Optimism
U-Understnding
N-Nurturance
S-Sharing
E-Empathy
L-Listening
I-Interest
N-Nourishing
G-Grace

While the mention of the term "Counseling" can be frightening when used on a formal basis, all Christians will eventually be called upon to use counseling skills when called to stand with those  in need suffering a crisis. Therefore, we should all be prepared to offer Godly Counseling in times of need and acute stress. Effective Crisis Care does not have to be a mystery, but occurs naturally when we act as caring Christians in a loving relationships of trust with others and God. If we seek divine wisdom with the confidence that the Holy Spirit or "Mighty Counselor" will draw along beside us and others in times of need, then Healing Counseling will naturally follow us, like day follows night. The Lord can use any Christian disciple for effective Crisis Care when we consciously surrender ourselves as vessels for the Healing Work of the Holy Spirit and consciously offer:

C-Concern

O-Optimism

U-Understanding

N-Nurturance

S-Sharing

E-Empathy

L-Listening

I-Interest

N-Nourishment

G-Grace

✓ *Questions For Individual Reflection*
Or Group Discussion

1. What is the biblical perspective on counseling according to the scriptures quoted in this chapter?

2. What biblical references concerning counseling in this chapter did you find especially important?

3. How do you feel at this point about ministering to someone in Crisis in light of the preceding information?

4. What areas or situations of potential Crisis Counseling do you currently feel confident in? What areas evoke anxiety?

CASE STUDY

John and Judy have been going to your church for the past three years. They are both well educated, have three teenage children, are faithful in church attendance, are serving well on various committees, and have expressed an interest in perhaps taking training as lay preachers. You have just received a phone call from John who is in the Emergency Room with Judy. He informs you that their 17 year old daughter has just been pronounced DOA (Dead On Arrival) after being hit by a drunk driver. He asks if you will come to the Emergency Room immediately.

1. How do you plan to provide Crisis Counseling and Pastoral Care to John and Judy and their family?

GROUP ACTIVITY

➤ 2. *Share your Crisis Plan with others or in a group for feedback and suggestions.*

Chapter 10: Mental Health Perspectives In Crisis Care

From mental health perspectives, a "Crisis" refers not to a specific traumatic event or experience, but to *how* individuals respond to acute stress. Most of us in extreme traumatic crisis develop a temporary "**Acute Stress Disorder**". We need to remember this occurs to many of us, in some degree, during or after a traumatic event or crisis involving possible physical or emotional trauma or injury to self or others. It is recognizable by responses involving some of the following:

- O A Sense of Detachment or Numbing during trauma or a Sense of Unreality such as "being in a daze"; lack of emotional response (flat affect), or over-responsiveness (hysteria).
- O A Traumatic event is followed eventually by marked symptoms of Anxiety or hyper-responsiveness involving difficulty sleeping, nightmares, guilt, poor concentration, hyper-vigilance, memory loss, irritability, exaggerated startle response, difficulty focusing, etc.
- O The Traumatic event is re-experienced with reminders of the trauma activating flashbacks, distress, recurrent thoughts, disturbing dreams, difficulties functioning efficiently, etc.

With proper intervention, support, and effective care, most Acute Stress Disorders resolve in time. The critical need for effective care for Acute Stress Disorders became apparent during WWI. In fact the origins of modern day Crisis Counseling dates back to World War I and World War II. Prior to this time, soldiers who exhibited significant psychological reactions to the acute stress experiences of war were frequently seen as "weak" or even disloyal. However, it soon became apparent that soldiers who were immediately offered treatment for acute stress disorders fared much better than their untreated counterparts. "Post Traumatic Stress Disorder" (PTSD) has since become recognized as partially the result of poor treatment and ineffective support during emotional crises for those with Acute Stress Disorder symptoms.

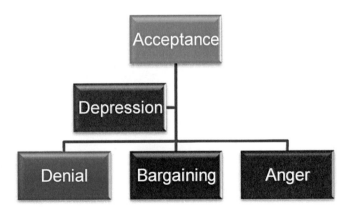

Since crisis brings loss, generally those in crisis will also exhibit the classic "**GRIEF STAGES**" Dr. Kubla-Ross described in her pioneering work on death and grief. These stages consist of: **Denial, Bargaining, Depression, Anger, and Acceptance.**

These phases do not occur in a neat linear order but usually bounce back and forth. Which phase one is currently "in" can best be determined by the current *primary* affect or emotion. However, there should generally be, over a period of time, a general movement towards "acceptance". If not, then complications may have occurred in the process of crisis resolution and often the individual will need some professional assistance to finally resolve the outstanding emotional issues. This is sometimes referred to as a state of "Complicated Bereavement." The events that trigger crisis can run the gamut of life experiences from acute emotional hurdles (such as occur when going through divorce or accidents), to natural disasters, to the death of loved ones. However, good "Crisis Care" always uses basic counseling skills to help individuals deal with the crisis by offering practical assistance and support.

DEVELOPING SKILLS IN GRIEF SUPPORT

While we all are eventually called at some time to reach out with comfort to those grieving, there are probably no skills more important in the difficult areas of Effective Grief Outreach than good supportive care and effective crisis intervention. This is achieved most effectively by: Listening, Prayer, and Good Communications. Our concentration on developing good abilities in these three areas, while using all the other resources our church and communities can offer, will give a sound foundation for expanding our spiritual gifts *and* skills in supporting others through crisis, grief and loss.

"Caring" from another is essential to grief recovery: Henri Nouwen, famous author and Catholic priest shared a profound truth with us in *The Wounded Healer* (1979, p.98) when he said, *"When we honestly ask ourselves which person in our lives means the most to us, we often find that it is those who, instead of giving much advice, solutions, or cures, have chosen rather to share our pain and touch our wounds with a gentle and tender hand. The friend who can be silent with us in a moment of despair or confusion, who can stay with us in an hour of grief and bereavement, who can tolerate not knowing, not curing, not healing and face with us the reality of our powerlessness-- that is, a friend who cares."*

Ultimately crisis care and ministry to those Grieving teaches us that we are all unique yet all similar. Yet no person experiences grief exactly as another person will. However, distress, sorrow, anguish and feelings of helplessness, weakness, and even hope are common to grief. The bible shows many different experiences of grief such as the ones following. Which of the passages from Psalms or Proverbs that are shown below speak to you most clearly?

- ⦿ **"Be merciful to me, O LORD, for I am in distress; my eyes grow weak with sorrow, my soul and my body with grief. My life is consumed by anguish and my years by groaning;" (Psalms 31:9-10; NIV)**

- ⦿ **"But you, God, see the trouble of the afflicted; you consider their grief and take it in hand. The victims commit themselves to you; you are the helper of the fatherless." (Psalms 10:14; NIV))**

✓ *Questions For Individual Reflection Or Group Discussion*

1. Which of the passages from Psalms above speaks to you most clearly?

2. Can you identify with the feelings of these writers? If so, how?

3. Above all, an experience of "Caring" seems vital for grief recovery. Does what Henri Nouwen say affect in any way how you would minister to another person who is in grief?

CASE STUDY

Martha has been a member of your church for 21 years. A week ago she lost her husband, George, after 52 years of marriage due to a stroke. After caring for him at home for a year, George's departure to be with the Lord was sudden, swift, and painfully traumatic. Martha keeps saying, "If only I had taken better care of George this would not have happened." She sobs uncontrollably and

 then sits in silence and is unresponsive to your efforts to comfort her. Martha then looks at you and says "If God really cared, he would have answered my prayers to take me first. I don't want to live without George." Martha is numb and unresponsive to your attempts to comfort her. She anxiously keeps re-arranging the newspapers on the couch during your visit.

1. *How will you provide crisis pastoral care to Martha? Include care for body, mind, soul, and spirit.*

GROUP ACTIVITY

2. *Share your plan with others or in a group for feedback and suggestions*

Chapter 11: Essential Steps In Crisis Care And Crisis Counseling

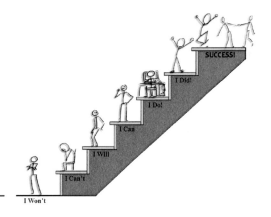

Crisis occurs when an acute situation exists requiring intervention for the health, safety, and welfare of those involved. Crisis counseling is intended to be quite brief, generally lasting for a period of no longer than a few weeks or sometimes even a few hours. It is important to note that crisis counseling is **not** psychotherapy. Crisis Intervention is focused on minimizing the stress of the event, providing emotional support and improving the individual's coping strategies in the here and now. Like psychotherapy, good Crisis Care, or professional Crisis Counseling, involves **assessment, planning, and treatment.** However, the scope of Crisis Care is generally much more specific and limited than professional counseling or psychotherapy. While psychotherapy focuses on a wide range of information and history, crisis assessment and treatment focuses on the individual's **immediate** situation. Factors such as safety and current needs are paramount. While there are a number of different treatment models, there are vital common elements consistent among the various theories of crisis care and crisis counseling. The nine "Essential Steps" in Crisis Care include:

1. Assessing the Situation: The first element of crisis counseling always involves *assessing* the individual's current crisis situation. This involves listening very carefully to the people involved, asking questions, and determining what they need to effectively cope with the crisis. During this time, the crisis care provider needs to *define the problem* while at the same time acting as a stable source of *empathy, acceptance, and support.* It

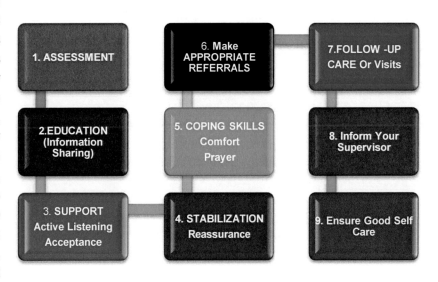

is also essential to ensure **safety**, both physically, spiritually, and emotionally. A tentative treatment plan is vital at this time that is appropriate for the situation.

2. Education: People who are experiencing a crisis may need **information** about their current condition and knowledge of the steps they can take to minimize the damage. During crisis care, trained care-givers often help individuals and families understand that their reactions are normal, but temporary. While the situation may seem both dire and endless to people experiencing the crisis, the goal is to help others see that he or she will eventually return to normal functioning. Or as scripture says, "Weeping endures for a season, but joy cometh in the morning". (Ps. 30:5; KJ) Available resources should be discussed such as warm clothing or temporary Red Cross housing available to families in fire loss.

3. Offering Support: One of the most important elements of crisis counseling involves offering **support, stabilization**, and **resources.** Active listening is critical, as well as sharing unconditional acceptance and reassurance. Offering this kind of **nonjudgmental support** during a crisis can help reduce stress and improves coping. During the crisis, it can be very beneficial for individuals to develop a brief dependency on supportive people. Unlike unhealthy dependencies, these time limited relationships help the individual become stronger and more independent.

4. Stabilization: Reassurance and accessing appropriate resources are vital to stabilize the crisis and prevent it from cascading into a permanent disaster. Care, food, shelter, safety, etc can be vital at this time. If the church or ministry does not have access to the needed resources, then good referrals should be given to places and people in the community that do have crisis resources. These can include homeless shelters, the Red Cross, Catholic Charities, community kitchens, food banks, battered women's shelters, Salvation Army, professional counseling, crisis suicide lines, location of emergency rooms, funeral homes, etc. Knowledge in these areas is vital.

5. Developing Coping Skills: In addition to providing support, crisis care givers also need to help individuals develop better coping skills to deal with the immediate crisis. This might involve helping the person explore different solutions to the problems, practicing stress reduction techniques, and encouraging positive thinking. This process is not just about teaching these skills to the person, it is also about demonstrating these skills and encouraging the individual to make a commitment to continue utilizing proper resources in the future. However, in a crisis nothing can substitute for prayer, bible reading, sustaining friendships, and assurance of support, faith, hope, and love.

6. Make Appropriate Referrals: There is no more critical skill in providing good crisis care than the ability to **make good and appropriate referrals**. Crisis Care and Crisis Counseling are, by definition, brief and should never exceed six visits and usually consists of two or three visits. During this time, your assessment of the situation should also include a long-term Treatment

Plan. Effective "Treatment Plans" include not only immediate assistance but also offering access to Long-Term Care and Support as needed. Know the names, locations, and phone numbers of Counseling Resources and Agencies in your area. Know the names and phone numbers and locations of Domestic Violence Shelters, Grief Support Groups, Care Giver Support Groups, AA and NA Groups, Funeral Home and Medical Care Sources, Food Pantries, etc. Written rather than verbal referrals are the most useful when someone is in shock or grief. When possible, two or more choices should be given in any one area of need so that a choice of counselors, funeral homes, support groups, etc. is possible for the individual experiencing crisis. United Way and Catholic Charities local offices are generally a very good source for quick and often free assistance including professional counseling for free or minimal fees.

7. Follow-Up Care: Some kind of follow up care should occur, with the permission of the individuals involved. A statement such as *"I will be contacting you later to see how you are doing. Is that OK?"* is appropriate. Follow-up care is vital to assure that isolation does not occur for the people in crisis and that a loving hand continues to reach out in their time of stress and shock. Crisis Care should be limited to no more than six visits or sessions. Anything beyond this becomes long-term care or counseling and is not appropriate. Further needs beyond six sessions indicate that professional help is needed and a referral needs to be made to appropriate agencies or mental health professionals at that time.

8. Inform Your Consultant and Senor Pastor or Supervisor about the crises as soon as possible. Review what you have done and develop further goals together. Discuss your overall treatment plan. Pastoral Care Team members should always inform the Senior Pastor right away of any crisis situation involving parishioners. Pastors, team members, and mental health professionals should always have collegial consultation in severe crises as the needs and stress can be overwhelming.

Good Self Care

9. Self Care: The importance of good self care cannot be emphasized enough for those who are involved in crisis care. Trauma is contagious and secondary post-traumatic stress disorder can occur. Find someone you can talk with who will keep all you might say as confidential. A supportive group is helpful while attendance at regular meetings of a Pastoral Care Support Team Group is essential to sustain involvement in the challenges of pastoral and crisis care. Develop good boundaries. Assure that you have time to play and seasons of rest and restoration or burnout can and will occur over time.

✓ *Questions For Individual Reflection Or Group Discussion*

1. Which of the 9 steps in Crisis Care discussed previously are you comfortable or uncomfortable with?

2. Which steps do you feel you would struggle with? Why?

3. How can you improve your own self care?

CASE STUDY

Your neighbor of 10 years, Jenny, appears at your front door crying and asks if she can come in and talk with you. You notice that her shirt is torn and her face is bruised. You ask if she is OK and inquire whether or not she has fallen. She responds, "No I didn't fall. Mike hit me," she sobs. "I am so scared. I don't know what to do. Can you help me?" Jenny has two grown sons that live out-of-town but she has few friends and seems isolated.

 1. Considering the nine steps discussed above, what is your treatment plan?

2. Utilize the Treatment Form Plan on the page following and specify what you will do to provide good Crisis Care.

3. GROUP ACTIVITY: *These Case Study questions may be completed either as a group or as an individual or both.*

CRISIS TREATMENT PLAN FORM

PROBLEM	IMMEDIATE ACTION	LONGTERM ACTION	RESULT

MEDITATION

"When the Son of Man comes in His glory, and all the holy angels with Him, then He will sit on the throne of His glory. ³² All the nations will be gathered before Him, and He will separate them one from another, as a shepherd divides *his* sheep from the goats. ³³ And He will set the sheep on His right hand, but the goats on the left.

³⁴ Then the King will say to those on His right hand, 'Come, you blessed of My Father, inherit the kingdom prepared for you from the foundation of the world: ³⁵ for I was hungry and you gave Me food; I was thirsty and you gave Me drink; I was a stranger and you took Me in; ³⁶ I *was* naked and you clothed Me; I was sick and you visited Me; I was in prison and you came to Me.'

³⁷ Then the righteous will answer Him, saying, 'Lord, when did we see you hungry and feed *you,* or thirsty and give *you* drink? ³⁸ When did we see you a stranger and take *you* in, or naked and clothe *you?* ³⁹ Or when did we see You sick, or in prison, and come to You?'

⁴⁰ And the King will answer and say to them, 'Assuredly, I say to you, inasmuch as you did *it* to one of the least of these My brethren, you did *it* to Me.' ⁴¹ Then He will also say to those on the left hand, 'Depart from Me, you cursed, into the everlasting fire prepared for the devil and his angels: ⁴² for I was hungry and you gave Me no food; I was thirsty and you gave Me no drink; ⁴³ I was a stranger and you did not take Me in, naked and you did not clothe Me, sick and in prison and you did not visit Me.'

⁴⁴ Then they also will answer Him, saying, 'Lord, when did we see You hungry or thirsty or a stranger or naked or sick or in prison, and did not minister to You?'

⁴⁵ Then He will answer them, saying, 'Assuredly, I say to you, inasmuch as you did not do it to one of the least of these, you did not do it to Me.' ⁴⁶ And these will go away into everlasting punishment, but the righteous into eternal life." (Matt. 25:31-46; NKJV)

✓ Questions for Individual Reflection

1. What are your goals at this point for a Ministry Team?

2. What role do you now hope to play in the ministry, community, or church?

3. What role do you currently hope you will play in the Ministry Team?

4. What kinds of ministry activities or types of pastoral care do you feel comfortable with now after completing this training in Crisis Care?

5. What kinds of Pastoral Care would you like to have more discussion or training about?

6. How do you currently feel about being part of a ministry support group?

7. If you are willing to be involved with a ministry team, when would be a good time to meet with others on a monthly basis?

8. What other topics are you looking forward to learning about in the areas of pastoral care and team ministries in the future?

9. What have you found most useful about this book?

10. *What do you feel are your own strengths and weaknesses in ministry and both pastoral and crisis care?*

GROUP ACTIVITIES AND QUESTIONS FOR RESOLUTION

11. How do you want your local ministry team specifically to be organized to be most effective in your current organizational structure?

12. What role(s) is each person in your group currently willing to play?

13. Does anyone feel called to any administrative or leadership roles in team ministry? If so who and what specifically?

14. What final steps are still needed to activate your local Ministry Team? What will each person do to help?

15. Make assignments to formalize and organize your team according to the gifts of each team member and their willingness to participate.

RESOURCES FOR FURTHER STUDY

BIBLIOGRAPY

RESOURCES FOR FURTHER STUDY

BIBLIOGRAPY

PASTORAL/CHRISTIAN COUNSELING AND CRISIS CARE

Adams, Jay E. *Competent To Counsel: Introduction to Nouthetic Counseling.*4012.2 Grand Rapids, MI: Zondervan Publishing House, 1986.

Collins, Gary, ed. *Helping People Grow:* Practical Approaches to Christian Counseling. Santa Ana, CA: Vision House, 1980.

.

Crabb, Lawrence J. Understanding People: Deep Longings for Relationship.4012.2 Grand Rapids, MI: Zondervan Publishing House, 1987.

Hiltner, Seward. *Pastoral Counseling*, Abingdon Press. 1982.

Johnson, Mary B. *Love In Action: The Healing Heritage Of The Counseling Ministry Of The Church.* U.S.A. Good News Publishing. 2013.

Johnson, Mary B. *Flying Free: Transforming Grief And Loss Into Renewal.* U.S.A. Good News Publishing, 2015.

Kottler, Jeffrey A. and Robert W. Brown. *Introduction To Therapeutic Counseling.* Monterey, CA: Brooks/Cole Publishing Co., 1985.

Nouwen, Henri J.M. *The Way of the Heart: Desert Spirituality and Contemporary Spirituality.* Ballantine Books, 1985.

Nouwen, Henri. *The Wounded Healer: Ministry in Contemporary Society.* New York: Image Books, Doubleday, 1979.

Oates, Wayne. *Protestant Pastoral Counseling.* Philadelphia: The Westminster Press, 1962.

O'Brien, Michael J. *An Introduction to Pastoral Counseling.* Staten Island, New York: Alba House, 1968.

Oglesby, William, Jr. *Biblical Themes for Pastoral Care.* Nashville: Abingdon, 1980.

*Wright, H. Norman. *Crisis Counseling: Helping People in Crisis and Stress.*4012.2 San Bernardino, CA: Here's Life Publishers, 1985. (Highly Recommended)

EMPOWERING LAY MINSTRY

P. Collins and R. P. Stevens, *The Equipping Pastor.* Washington, D.C.: Alban Institute, 1993.

L. Doohan, *The Lay-Centered Church: Theology and Spirituality.* Minneapolis: Winston, 1984.

M. Gibbs and T. Ralph Morton, *God's Frozen People.* London: Fontana Books, 1964.

B. Hull, *The Disciple-Making Pastor.* Old Tappan, N.J.: Fleming H. Revell, 1988.

G. Martin and L. Richards, *Lay Ministry: Empowering the People of God* .Grand Rapids: Zondervan, 1981.

G. Ogden, *The New Reformation: Returning the Ministry to the People of God*. Grand Rapids: Zondervan, 1990.

J. H. Ok, *Called to Awaken the Laymen*. Seoul, Korea: Tyrannus Press, 1984.

W. J. Rademacher, *Lay Ministry: A Theological, Spiritual and Pastoral Handbook*. New York: Crossroad, 1991.

Ronch, Judah: *The Counseling Sourcebook: A Practical Reference on Contemporary Issues*. Cokesbury: Crossroads, 1993.

A. Rowthorn, *The Liberation of the Laity*. Wilton, Conn.: Morehouse-Barlow, 1986.

R. E. Slocum, *Maximize Your Ministry: How You as a Lay Person Can Impact Your World for Jesus Christ*. Colorado Springs: NavPress, 1986.

M. J. Steinbron, *Can the Pastor Do It Alone? A Model for Preparing Lay People for Lay Pastoring*. Ventura, Calif.: Regal, 1987.

R. P. Stevens, *The Equipper's Guide to Every-Member Ministry*. Downers Grove, Ill: InterVarsity Press, 1992.

R. P. Stevens, *Liberating the Laity* (Downers Grove, Ill.: Inter Varsity Press, 1985);

H. W. Stone, *The Caring Church: A Guide for Lay Pastoral Care*. San Francisco: Harper & Row, 1983.

F. R. Tillapaugh, *Unleashing the Church*. Ventura, Calif.: Regal, 1982.

J. H. Yoder, *The Fullness of Christ: Paul's Vision of Universal Ministry*. Elgin, Ill.: Brethren Press, 1987.

ARTICLES

A. Christensen and N. S. Jacobson, "Who (or What) Can Do Psychotherapy: The Status and Challenge of Nonprofessional Therapies," Psychological Science 5 (1994) 8-14.

G. R. Collins, "Lay Counseling Within The Local Church," Leadership 1, no. 4 (1980) 78-86.

J. D. Frank, "Therapeutic Components Shared by All Psychotherapies," in Psychotherapy Research and Behavior Change, ed. J. H. Harvey and M. M. Parks (Washington, D.C.: American Psychological Association, 1982) 9-37.

Janice K. Kiecolt-Glaser, "Chronic stress and age-related increases in the proinflammatory cytokine IL", (Department of Psychology, University of North Carolina, Chapel Hill, NC). 2003.

M. J. Lambert and A. E. Bergin, "The Effectiveness of Psychotherapy," in *Handbook of Psychotherapy and Behavior Change*, ed. A. E. Bergin and S. L. Garfield (4th ed., New York: Wiley, 1994) 143-189.

R. P. Lorion and R. D. Felner, "Research on Mental Health Interventions with the Disadvantaged," in *Handbook of Psychotherapy and Behavior Change,* ed. S. L. Garfield and A. E. Bergin (3rd ed. New York: Wiley, 1986) 739-775.

D. M. Stein and M. J. Lambert, "Graduate Training in Psychotherapy: Are Therapy Outcomes Enhanced?" Journal of Consulting and Clinical Psychology 63 (1995) 182-196.

J. Sturkie and S. Y. Tan, *Advanced Peer Counseling in Youth Groups* (Grand Rapids: Zondervan/Youth Specialties, 1993).

 J. Sturkie and S. Y. Tan, *Peer Counseling in Youth Groups*. Grand Rapids: Zondervan/Youth Specialties, 1992) 431-440.

S. Y. Tan, "Development and Supervision of Paraprofessional Counselors," in *Innovations in Clinical Practice: A Sourcebook*, ed. L. Vande Creek, S. Knapp and T. L. Jackson. Sarasota, Fla.: Professional Resource, 1992.

S. Y. Tan, *Lay Counseling: Equipping Christians for a Helping Ministry*. Grand Rapids: Zondervan, 1991.

The *Archives Of Family Medicine:* 1998, Nov.-Dec.

Versions of the English Bible

HCSB *Holman Christian Standard Bible*. Nashville, Tennessee: Holman Bible Publishers, 2004.

KJ *King James or Authorized Version*. New York: World, 1950.

NAS *New American Standard.* LaHabra, California: World, 1973.

NIV *New International Version*. Grand Rapids: Zondervan, 1974. 1984. 2003.

RSV *Revised Standard Version*. New York: Oxford Press, 1965.

ABOUT THE AUTHOR

The author of *Activating The Power Of Pastoral Care: A Team Approach,* Rev. Dr. Mary Johnson, D.Min, has served as an Ordained Minister since 1975, both as a Parish Pastor and in multiple Specialized Ministry Settings. She has diverse experiences as a gifted author, seminar leader, parish pastor, preacher, chaplain, teacher, clinical counselor, clinical supervisor and adjunct college professor. She is skilled in pastoral training, consultation, clinical evaluations, psychological assessments, DSM clinical diagnosis, treatment planning, and individual, family, marital, and group counseling, supervision, and training.

Rev. Johnson has extensive pastoral experience and has held pastoral positions in Congregational, Methodist, Independent, and Assembly of God churches and is currently preaching in various denominational churches in New England. Dr. Johnson has worked on the Clinical Staff of New England Memorial Hospital and Middleton Pastoral Counseling Center in Massachusetts and was a Director of Renew and Green Pastures Counseling Centers in N.H. She has also served in Hospital Chaplaincy at Holy Family Hospital in Methuen, MA and Tewksbury State Hospital in Massachusetts. She was appointed to the Clinical and Supervisory Staff for the training of Chaplain Interns while at Tewksbury where she also worked as a Clinical Pastoral Education (CPE) Supervisor. While serving as  Executive Director at Good News Ministries, Inc., she was also appointed to the Adjunct Faculties of Antioch New England Graduate School, Gordon Conwell Seminary, Keene State, Goddard College, and the University of New Hampshire while training graduate level counselors and counseling ministers. Currently, Dr. Johnson is serving as a Consultant to various churches and ministries including Good News Specialized Ministries, Inc. in NH. After Dr. Johnson founded Good News, this unique ministry provided education and Clinical Christian Counseling to thousands of people over the decades and trained numerous Clinical Counselors and Counseling Ministers while offering weekly non-denominational worship services to the community until 2005. The current emphasis of Good News, Inc. is educational in nature.

Dr. Johnson has been included in "Who's Who Among Human Services Professionals" and "Who's Who In Religion." She has earned credentials as a state Licensed Clinical Mental Health Counselor, Nationally Board Certified Counselor (N.C.C.), and Nationally Certified Pastoral Counselor (AAPC) and also held certification as a Clinical Member of the Association for Clinical Pastoral Education (A.C.P.E.). Dr. Johnson was instrumental in developing and ensuring passage of the original NH certification/licensure law that also guaranteed the right of pastors to counsel members of their congregation.

Her Doctor of Ministry Degree in Psychology and Clinical Studies from Andover Newton in Newton, Mass. is unique in its integrative emphasis on psychology, clinical work, and theology. A Th.M., cum laude, from Boston University School of Theology combined a Dual Integrative Major in Pastoral Counseling and Biblical Studies. A B.S., cum laude, from Black Hills State University in Spearfish, South Dakota integrated a Major in History with Minors in Political Science and Education. She has also studied at the Kansas City Art Institute, American University in Washington, D.C., and The College of Emporia in Kansas. Her early training was as a commercial artist. She has exhibited in numerous art shows and received multiple awards for her paintings and other art work after being accepted as a member of the National Art Honor Society.

Both Dr. Johnson's life-long devotion to a Healing Ministry and her love for people are apparent in all her work and writings. She has a strong love of family, poetry, nature, art, painting, writing, gardening, and God's people. While born in West Virginia, she was raised in Oklahoma and Kansas. After marrying an Air Force career officer, their assignments included Texas, California, South Dakota, New York, and New Hampshire. Today she is active preaching, consulting, writing, teaching, leading seminar presentations, and also enjoying a team ministry with her husband, now a NH Methodist pastor. They do worship services, workshops, seminars, and special events together, enjoy writing original songs, and recently co-authored the popular book *"Following The Angel Trail: In The Steps Of Jesus."* Dr. Johnson enjoys illustrating and designing her own books and looks forward to completing many more books now in process as she anticipates the future.

Dr. Johnson is the author of five other published books currently available online at either the amazon.com bookstore or for pickup at Barnes and Noble after advance order. These books include: *Flying Free: Transforming Grief and Loss into Renewal"; Following The Angel Trail: In The Steps Of Jesus"; "Love In Action: The Healing Heritage Of The Counseling Ministry Of The Church"; "Visions Of Hope: Voices Of Americana";* and *"Healing Streams".* She has also been published in the AAPC professional Journal "Journeys" and in the Keene Sentinel.

BOOKS BY REV. DR. MARY JOHNSON

These books may be purchased online at the amazon.com bookstore by going to the "Mary B. Johnson" Authors Page on Amazon at **http://www.amazon.com/Mary-B.-Johnson/e/B00EPHVW1K/ref=ntt_dp_epwbk_0**

__Flying Free: Transforming Grief And Loss Into Renewal__ "This treasure of a book by Dr. Mary Johnson offers invaluable practical guidance on transforming grief and loss into renewal. Written from the heart by an experienced clinical counselor, pastor, and psychotherapist, it comprehensively covers ways to heal emotions, body, mind, spirit, and soul after traumas of loss and grief. *"Flying Free: Transforming Grief And Loss Into Renewal"* brings both healing and hope in times of loss and bereavement. It also offers proven recovery methods from large varieties of loss including not only death of those we love but also offers successful ways to heal from divorce, separation, unemployment, loss of health, etc. If you have ever experienced a significant loss, this book is a "must read". **6x9 Paperback: 214 pages; Published: October 14, 2015**

__Following The Angel Trail: In The Steps Of Jesus__ co-authored with Pastor Arnie Johnson. This book "reads like a gripping detective novel yet reveals the often hidden history of Jesus including shepherds, prophets, evil kings, angels, innkeepers, Wise Men, his own extensive family, and many others. A Timeline, extensive Study Guide, Maps, comprehensive Endnotes, excellent resources for group or individual Bible Study, and excellent scholarship make this beautifully written and illustrated book both a bargain and great treasure. A real page turner and compelling read you will not want to put down!" -C. Barber, RN.
6x9 Paperback: 236 pages; Published: October 24, 2014

__Love In Action: The Healing Heritage Of The Counseling Ministry Of The Church__
"As a Methodist pastor I am riveted by this fascinating book by Rev. Dr. Mary Jonson exploring the 'Healing Heritage of The Counseling Ministry Of The Church'. This book is a monumental achievement and offers a fresh integrated perspective for anyone interested in Holistic Healing, counseling, or pastoral counseling. Ministers, counselors, nurses, physicians, therapists, pastors, social workers, and lay people will find this superb scholarly work both a page turner AND an invaluable guide and lively practical resource for diverse healing ministries. I cannot recommend it enough! A must book for your library! "-Pastor E. Davis, MTS, M.Div.
7 x 10 Paperback: 302 pages; Published: October 18, 2013

__Healing Streams: Journeys Of Healing__ "Healing Streams" is a unique combination of beautiful poetry and a study guide to assist those struggling to heal from an illness-physical, mental, emotional or spiritual. The poems speak of ordinary events in peoples' live that are easy for the reader to identify with. The poems, along with the Study Guide for Healing, offer hope and practical solutions with specific ways to find a healthier future for both yourself and loved ones. Beautifully written and illustrated!" -Andrea Galbraith on July 16, 2009.
 7 x 0.2 x 10 Paperback: 100 pages; Published: December 18, 2008

__Visions Of Hope: Voices Of Americana__ "This book is an inspiring poetic journey through the by-ways of a forgotten Americana that leaves the reader hope filled and appreciative of the rich heritage we all share in our country. Dr. Johnson's skills in graphic arts and the inclusion of stunning original colored photographs makes this a book to be treasured for its inspirational insights and ability to bring a renewed understanding of how we can all make a better tomorrow for ourselves and our country. By exploring the by-ways of our land and looking back to the values of forgotten times, new direction is found in this work by the reader for an inviting future of hope-filled better days ahead for all of us."
6 x 0.2 x 9 Paperback: 82 pages; Published: March 14, 2008

INDEX

INDEX

Notes And Reflections

Notes And Reflections

שָׁלוֹם

SHALOM